936.13

Cirencester College Library
Fosse Way Campus
Stroud Road
Cirencester
GL7 1XA

DISCOVERING THE NEOLITHIC IN COUNTY KERRY

D1335808

Cirencester College, GL7 1XA
CIRENCESTER COLLEGE LIBRARY
Telephone: 01285 640994
WITHDRAWN FROM STOCK

331771

Discovering the Neolithic in County Kerry:

a passage tomb at Ballycarty

Michael Connolly

First published in 1999
Wordwell Ltd
PO Box 69, Bray, Co. Wicklow
Copyright © Wordwell 1999.

All rights reserved. No part of this book may be reprinted or reproduced or utilised in any electronic, mechanical or other means, now known or hereafter invented, including photocopying and recording, or otherwise without either the prior written consent of the publishers or a licence permitting restricted copying in Ireland issued by the Irish Copyright Licensing Agency Ltd, The Writers' Centre, 19 Parnell Square, Dublin 1.

Cover design: Ger Garland

ISBN 1 869857 30 5

British Library Cataloguing-in-Publication Data.
A catalogue record for this book is available from the British Library.

Typeset in Ireland by Wordwell Ltd.
Book design: Jen Brady and Nick Maxwell.
Origination by Wordwell Ltd.

Printed by Brookfield Printing Company

Contents

Foreword

The categorisation and interpretation of the intriguing monument at Ballycarty are not helped by the degree to which its contents have been disturbed, particularly in the third phase of its use. The original burials included a cremated adult male, which, taken with the finds assemblage (in particular the antler disc bead, the slug knife and the scrapers), suggests a late Neolithic date consistent with passage tomb culture. Some of the structural features identified at Ballycarty, in particular the curved phase 2 façade, are unusual among passage tombs, as indeed is the site's outlying position in their distribution map. However, whatever way you look at this remarkable monument, it does relate to passage tomb traditions, although perhaps not in itself a classic Irish expression of the type.

It doesn't really matter all that much, except to archaeologists, whether Ballycarty is a classic passage tomb or not. What matters is that, thanks to these excavations, we now have for the first time a funerary monument of Neolithic date and type in an area of Ireland where Stone Age monuments appeared to be non-existent. Discoveries of this period and type show that we are really only at the beginning of Stone Age studies in Ireland. Only in the last half-century have they been put on a scientific footing, and the main tomb types have been categorised more recently than that. The ascription of the pottery and related assemblages to the tomb types is more recent still, and the balanced use of radiocarbon dating is still in progress.

That the Ballycarty tomb rattles our perceived confidence about tomb types shows the Irish Neolithic to be as exciting as the beginning of any study. The disturbance of the funerary/burial evidence and the consequential impossibility of reliable dating evidence in the case of this tomb make the whole thing intriguing and argue for the extension of what has been to date a most rewarding excavation campaign in the vale of Tralee.

One of the most noteworthy features of this excavation report is the importance accorded to the whole context of the landscape in which the tomb was located. By highlighting the chronologically related—and even unrelated—monuments in the same place rather than focusing tightly on the initial target of his excavations the author has literally broadened our horizons and our expectations. We have been taken beyond the mere site to its wider location, and beyond the relatively narrow time-frame of the monument's use (although three different phases of evidence were found in the excavation) to the ongoing significance of this outcrop and related area to people over a considerable span of time. All the more surprising, then, that the site was not located or identified until 1996, and surprising too that its significance as a place of ancient burial or general antiquity did not survive into modern folklore.

It is for me a cause for personal celebration that the excavator/author is first and foremost a museum man. The recent enforced retreat of museum archaeologists to what many less practical archaeologists believe to be their proper indoor habitat is to be deplored. Surely the more generally experienced the practitioner is in all aspects of the subject—excavation, survey, artefact study, cataloguing, rescue, teaching, scientific back-up and publication—the better he/she will be. The more varied the experience of the museum curator, in a local or national institution, the fuller the story at the museum and the fitter the curator to communicate the story in all its contexts. And that is not to mention the educational, political and publicity value of the curator being seen to be actively engaged with the broadest public beyond the walls of the institution. In Kerry, there is the additional asset of responsibly exploiting an ancient site with the positive aim of developing it as an educational and tourist attraction.

I am delighted to commend this site and the report of its excavator, the County Museum curator Michael Connolly, to the widest public, and I wish Kerry County Council well in their future work at the site.

Rath Dé ar an obair.

Patrick F. Wallace,
Director, National Museum of Ireland.

Preface

This book presents the results of a sixteen-week excavation in the townland of Ballycarty, 3.5km east of Tralee, Co. Kerry. The excavation and the publication of this book were funded entirely by Kerry County Council, and every courtesy and facility were extended to the excavation team by the staff of the Council.

The results of the excavation, and indeed the detailed survey of the limestone 'reef' on which the excavation took place, were startling, and in turn led to a short, intensive field survey of selected areas of the valley of the River Lee, from Ballycarty westward to Tralee Bay. This survey work was carried out from May to October 1997 and was funded by a grant from the National Monuments Section of *Dúchas* The Heritage Service.

If the results of the small excavation at Ballycarty were startling, the results of the field survey of the Lee Valley were extraordinary. This fieldwork has continued intermittently, and at the time of publication of this book over 100 previously unrecorded archaeological sites have been identified. A number of these were extensive complexes, containing up to fourteen separate elements, many situated on or around limestone 'reefs' similar to Ballycarty. Very recently a probable third hillfort has been identified, while geophysical survey of an embanked enclosure indicates that there is deposited metal and a possible central post in its interior.

The majority of these sites are of prehistoric type, and their discovery makes the Lee Valley the major prehistoric landscape in the county. Indeed, complexes such as those at Annagh and Ballycarty would compare favourably with the finest examples elsewhere in the country.

Research into the sites of the Lee Valley will continue and, hopefully, funding for specialised investigation will be made available. As things now stand, the possibilities are intriguing.

Whatever future fieldwork and research may uncover, the impetus to look again at the archaeology of this area of County Kerry came from the excavations at Ballycarty, which revealed Ireland's most westerly passage tomb.

Acknowledgements

The author would like to express his thanks to the following: Kerry County Council, in particular the staff of the Roads Design Section, for their cooperation and assistance during the excavation and for covering the costs of this publication; Mr Tom Condit of the National Monuments Service, Mr Paul Walsh of the Ordnance Survey and Professor Etienne Rynne for their advice and comments on the site; Professor Peter Woodman, Ms Margaret McCarthy, Ms Catryn Power, Mr John Tierney and Dr Patrick Wyse Jackson for the various specialist reports; Mr Tom Condit and Mr John Sheehan for their comments on the text; Mr Frank Coyne for preparing the illustrations in the book, his work on the excavation, his comments on the text and his perceptive fieldwork; Mr Lar Dunne for photographing the finds from the excavation and allowing me to use information from his excavations at Cloghers, Tralee, Co. Kerry; and Ms Sandra Leahy for working on the figures in the text. Finally I would like to thank the archaeological team who worked so hard to excavate the site to the highest standards possible.

For Marie and Niall

1. INTRODUCTION

County Kerry has long been noted for its wealth of Early Christian remains, yet while it also contains high densities of certain prehistoric site types—standing stones, alignments, stone circles and rock art—as well as evidence for early copper-mining and the late Mesolithic site at Ferriter's Cove, its prehistoric archaeological record is contradictory and prone to large gaps.

Not so long ago it was generally accepted that Kerry, in particular the peninsular areas, was uninhabited until the Bronze Age, but work at Cashelkeelty on the Beara Peninsula produced evidence for early cereal cultivation (Lynch 1981, 83), while the excavations at Ferriter's Cove clearly indicated settlement as early as 5620 BP (Woodman *et al.* 1984, 5–8).

While such discoveries have altered our perception of prehistory in the south-west of the country, they have also served to highlight the long gaps in the archaeological record of the county and have provided us with many unanswered questions, such as 'Where did the people who were obviously living around Cashelkeelty and Ferriter's Cove at the time of the Mesolithic/Neolithic transition go?'

Indeed, this raises the whole question of the evidence for the Neolithic in Kerry and the contradictions provided by the evidence for Bronze Age settlement. Neolithic artefacts, while not numerous, are known from the county, and work on Valentia Island indicated land clearance around 5000 BP, as well as walls and stone trackways of Neolithic date (Mitchell 1989, 94–5).

Yet where was the wider settlement evidence, and more particularly the burial evidence? The question of clear settlement evidence was not peculiar to Kerry, as its survival is often dependent on many factors. However, the accumulating evidence for early cereal cultivation and the artefact record made the lack of burial evidence more puzzling.

The excavations at Ballycarty and the discovery of a passage tomb may partially answer this question, and open many avenues of speculation regarding the numerous unopened cairns both in the immediate area of Ballycarty and in the county as a whole. Indeed, the possibility that Ballycarty is but one tomb within a small passage tomb cemetery cannot be ignored, while recent work on cairns in other parts of the county, most notably the pair which sit on the summits of 'The Paps' in east Kerry (Frank Coyne, pers. comm.), suggests that this site type may have a wide distribution within the county.

It is also notable that recent work on the southern side of Tralee has uncovered the remains of a Neolithic house and has produced both flint artefacts and Western Neolithic pottery (Lar Dunne, pers. comm.), while a range of sites—henges, a cursus, barrows and embanked enclosures—of probable Neolithic and Early Bronze Age date have been identified in the Tralee area.

A recently identified cave system containing at least four disarticulated, partially burnt burials at Cloghermore, 2km north-east of Ballycarty, may well prove to be the source of further prehistoric burial evidence.

Indeed, excavations on the northern side of Tralee, on the south-facing slope of a low ridge which runs west from the Stacks Mountains to Tralee Bay, have provided the best evidence for Bronze Age burial in the county, with the discovery of a number of cremation burials in shallow pits.

It is interesting that these burials should occur in the area that divides the northern and eastern quadrants of the county, with their concentrations of Bronze Age artefacts, from the peninsulas and the high densities of Bronze Age site types. In fact the predominance of Later Bronze Age material in the northern half of the county and the occurrence of most of the Early Bronze Age hoards in the southern half may indicate a temporal as well as a geographical division, and one between site and artefact.

Given the Late Bronze Age origins proposed for hillforts, it is surely no accident that the bivallate hillfort of Glanbane, 5.5km to the east of Ballycarty, and the recently identified bivallate hillfort at Lohercannan, 5km to the west, sit in the foothills of the Slieve Mish, which form the geographical barrier between the north and south of the county.

This brings us back to the original question of where the people who settled at Ferriter's Cove and began land clearance and cereal cultivation on the western margins of the county went. It is approximately 60km along the northern side of the Dingle Peninsula from Ferriter's Cove to the fertile, sheltered Lee Valley, with its protected bay. It is not too difficult to make the journey intellectually, and only slightly more so on foot. It would seem improbable that these early settlers did not travel this short distance inland and find in the Lee Valley an area suitable for the development of a Neolithic society, while the excavations at Ballycarty and subsequent survey work clearly indicate that such a society did develop and continued into the Bronze Age.

This book presents the results of the excavations at Ballycarty leading to the discovery of Europe's most westerly passage tomb. It attempts to place the tomb within the Irish and European series and briefly discusses the implications for the distribution, dating and developmental sequence of Irish passage tombs. The results of subsequent survey work are outlined and the implications for our understanding of the prehistory of the south-west are briefly discussed.

However, the available information raises as many questions as it answers, and while some of the speculations offered in the text may prove to be correct, only further excavation and research will provide definitive answers.

Until then, anything is possible!

2. GEOGRAPHICAL SETTING

As part of the preparations for the construction of the new link road (N22) between Ballycarty Cross and the Killarney road, the Office of Public Works requested trial excavations on a portion of the proposed route through the townland of Ballycarty, 4km east of Tralee (OS 6" Sheet 38, Barony of Trughanacmy, Parish of Ballyseedy, coordinates 810mm east, 592mm north, National Grid reference Q871 123). The excavation was undertaken by a team of fourteen archaeologists, under the auspices of the Roads Design Section of Kerry County Council, over fourteen weeks during the summer of 1996.

The lands in question were situated on the west-facing slope of a limestone (Waulsortian) reef which runs for approximately 200m from the east, westward toward Tralee. The spur is one of the highest points on the floor of the broad, flat valley formed by the Stacks Mountains to the north-north-east and the Slieve Mish to the south-south-west. The River Lee rises in the Stacks Mountains and flows southward to the valley floor before curving sharply to the west on its course to the sea at Blennerville. The river is fed by streams from both mountain ranges.

The central location of the spur, close to the broad bend of the river, affords expansive views in all directions, including the most accessible passes through the flanking mountains and two fording-points on the River Lee.

The low-lying land around the spur is recorded on early maps as being marshy and this would have given the spur all the appearance of a promontory, the only dry approach being from the east. Aerial photography appears to indicate that the area around the spur was reclaimed, and this is substantiated by the current landowner and by the OS 1st edition map.

The spur itself is composed of Carboniferous limestone with a minimal soil cover and contains an extraordinary wealth of fossil evidence. The maximum height of the spur is 32m above sea-level (OD), while the maximum height of the area under investigation is 29.5m.

The OS 6" and 25" 1st edition maps for the area, as well as the Sites and Monuments Record for County Kerry, recorded an enclosure centrally placed on the limestone spur. However, a survey of the spur indicated a far more complex site than was previously realised.

SITE DESCRIPTION (Pl. 1; Fig. 1)

The features on the reef consist of six main elements: (1) the ramparts, (2) the causeway, (3) smaller enclosures, (4) the hilltop enclosure or henge, (5) quarry ditches, and (6) the cairns. The area of excavation will be described separately as the seventh element of the site.

(1) The ramparts

The northern side of the reef is enclosed by at least two collapsed stone and earth ramparts, clearly visible at ground level. A possible third rampart can be seen on some aerial photographs but is unidentifiable at ground level. There are also traces of a wide ditch between the two visible ramparts. Only a single rampart can be seen on the southern side, but since the reef is much lower here any further defences would probably have been built on the level land below the reef, and may well have been destroyed during reclamation. Indeed, the marshy nature of the land prior to reclamation may have been deemed sufficient defence for the southern side of the reef (Pl. 2).

The ramparts are continuous along the western half of the reef but become intermittent and difficult to identify from the mid-point of the spur to its eastern extent. Over most of their length they have been built on the natural breaks in the slope and scarped back into

3

the reef; however, toward the eastern end of the reef the rampart on the northern side takes the form of a bank, while the southern side alternates between the scarped construction and a bank feature.

The ditch, between the two ramparts on the northern side, is most clearly visible along the eastern half of the reef. It is very shallow, 0.3–0.4m in depth, and has an average width of 3.73m. If this depression does in fact denote a ditch, then it is likely to be rock-cut and has most probably filled up with slipped material from the inner rampart.

Initially no trace of these ramparts could be seen on the western or eastern ends of the spur, but sod-stripping later revealed the rampart at the western end. A similar undertaking may well expose a rampart cutting off the eastern end of the reef and fill in the gaps in the more intermittent stretches. It also appears likely that some of the many structures at the eastern end of the spur utilise the rampart line, and possibly the rampart itself, as part of their construction.

The maximum external height of the rampart where it takes the form of an enhanced scarp is 0.8m, with a maximum width of 3.8m. Where this scarp changes to a conventional bank it has a maximum external height of 0.57m, an internal height of 0.44m and a width of 3.3m.

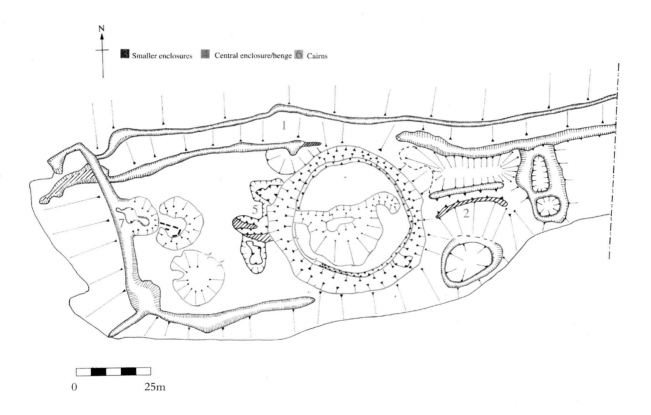

Fig. 1—Plan of the archaeological features on the limestone reef at Ballycarty.

Pl. 1—The limestone reef at Ballycarty from the west.

Pl. 2—The limestone reef from the north-west—two of the ramparts on the north side of the reef can be seen inside the fence line.

The maximum length of the conventional bank, on the northern side, is 39.5m, while the distance between the double rampart, where it can be defined on the ground, is on average 5.8m.

These meandering ramparts enclose an area with minimum measurements of 88m north–south and 200m east–west, covering approximately 1.76 hectares.

(2) The causeway

The eastern end of the spur is the most complicated area of the site. Here the rampart that encloses the rest of the site is not visible on the surface, but a number of other features at this end may be utilising or obscuring its line. The main feature at the eastern end is an embanked causeway-like structure which runs east–west from the level land at the eastern end of the spur right up to the wall of the central enclosure.

The north side of the causeway is formed by a bank of earth and stone, utilising the plane of the existing bedrock outcrops, while the southern side is formed predominantly of bedrock outcrop, again augmented by stone and earth. These banks are on average 0.7m high internally, 1.3m high externally and 4m wide.

Internally the causeway has a U-shaped profile and is 4.5m in maximum width. The banks on either side are parallel-sided and the total length of the structure is 23m. This feature shows up very well on aerial photographs, and while it has the appearance of some form of causeway or entrance through the enclosing rampart, further investigation would be needed to confirm its exact function.

(3) The smaller enclosures

Immediately abutting the northern bank of this causeway-like feature is a subcircular depression which seems to have been formed by the convergence of the main rampart, the central enclosure and the northern bank of the causeway feature. It measures 7.2m north–south, 11.5m east–west, and has an average depth of 0.55m.

Immediately to the south of the causeway is the most easterly feature on the spur. This small, subcircular enclosure shows up very clearly on aerial photography but is much harder to define at ground level. The enclosing bank is most clearly defined to the south, where it is 3.7m wide and has an average height of 0.3m. The northern side of the enclosure is formed by the convergence of this horseshoe-shaped bank with the southern side of the causeway-like feature and the natural scarp of the spur. Since the causeway bank is built on a higher terrace of the spur, the northern side of this small enclosure is very steep, with an average height of 0.6m. The feature measures 20m north–south by 21.3m east–west externally and 12.5m north–south by 13.5m east–west internally.

The final two features on the eastern end of the spur lie directly outside the eastern end of the causeway and take the form of two conjoined subcircular enclosures. The more northerly of the two measures 16.8m north–south by 13.7m east–west externally and 11.5m north–south by 5.4m east–west internally. The enclosing bank is completely sod-covered and very denuded, remaining only to an average height of 0.33m, with an average width of 4.6m. The more southerly enclosure is less clearly defined but appears to be subcircular. Again the bank is very low. The feature measures 10.2m north–south by 12m east–west externally and 6.2m north–south by 5.9m east–west internally. The average width of the bank is 3.5m.

(4) The hilltop enclosure or henge (Pl. 3)

The only feature on the reef recorded on previous maps and in the SMR for County Kerry is the central enclosure (OS 6" Sheet 38, SMR No. Ke038 022). The enclosure has a

Pl. 3—The central hengiform enclosure.

substantial earth and stone bank all round, except for a gap at least 7m long, and possibly as long as 25m, on the northern side where the natural scarp of the hill falls away from the site, giving this side the appearance of a raised platform.

Whether or not the bank ever existed at this point is hard to say, but the presence of a natural scarp here suggests that this was not the site of an entrance. The bank encloses an area measuring 39m north–south and 38m east–west, and has a maximum width of 7.6m on its southern side. It has an average height of 0.6m internally and 0.75m externally. The causeway feature, already described, runs right up to the enclosing bank on the eastern side.

Inside the bank there is a very definite internal ditch, 1.6m wide and with an average depth of 0.34m. It would appear to be at least partially rock-cut and is visible all round the site except in the south-western quadrant, where it may be obscured by collapse from the rampart.

Eccentrically placed inside the enclosure or henge is a subcircular sod-covered cairn of stone measuring 22.6m north–south by 22m east–west, with a maximum height of 1.5m. The surface of the cairn exhibits a P-shaped area of collapse, 6.5m in total length and 2.5m in width, with an average depth of 0.5m.

Running east and west from this central mound is a stone and earth bank, on average 4m wide and 0.35m high. On the western side this feature runs right up to the enclosing bank, but on the eastern side it stops 3.6m short of it. The bank on the western side is almost perfectly straight, while that running from the eastern side has a distinct curvature.

Pl. 4—The exposed chamber and passage of a second cairn, immediately east of the excavated site.

(5) The quarry ditches

Immediately outside and abutting the western side of the central enclosure are four large, subrectangular, rock-cut depressions. The most northerly example measures 7.4m by 12m and has an average depth of 0.5m. The second pit measures 10m by 4m and has an average depth of 0.7m. The third measures 4.8m by 1.8m by 0.5m deep, while the most southerly example measures 9m by 7.9m by 0.75m deep. Their exact function is impossible to ascertain, but they may be quarry ditches associated with some phase of the construction on the reef.

(6) The cairns

The final two features, lying immediately east of the limit of the excavation, appear to be stone cairns. The more northerly of the two is very denuded and its central area is exposed. Here, large boulders and bedrock outcrop appear to denote the line of a 3.1m-long passage leading to a large, subcircular, rock-cut chamber, 1.6m north–south by 2.2m east–west. The surviving cairn is visible all round this exposed central area. The site measures 16.5m north–south by 11.9m east–west (Pl. 4).

The more southerly example could very easily pass for a natural terrace of the spur, but the large stones visible intermittently around its western side may be evidence of a kerb, and the material forming this feature seems to consist of loose stone and earth which has been built up against a natural scarp on the spur. The site has approximate dimensions of 26.2m north–south by 19.4m east–west.

(7) The area of excavation

Within the area affected by the roadway, survey revealed the presence of a low, subcircular mound, 11m north–south by 8.7m east–west, surviving to a height of 0.53m. Centrally placed on the mound was a shallow, P-shaped depression measuring 2m north–south, 4.6m east–west and 0.17m deep. The mound seemed to have a sunken, semicircular, court-like feature on its western side, which connected with the P-shaped depression on the mound. The northern side of this court feature seemed to consist of a stone and earth bank, while on the southern side the tops of four large stones could be seen (Fig. 2).

Sod-stripping exposed a previously unseen section of rampart which ran right across the western end of the spur, linking with the previously recorded rampart on the southern side but running over that on the northern side and downslope to the surrounding lowland, where it terminated abruptly. The rampart abutted what was now very obviously a low stone and earth cairn on its southern side and then curved sharply to go around the front of the cairn, effectively sealing the court. It was very collapsed and was composed of earth and stone. It remained to an average external height of 0.46m and was on average 3m wide (Pl. 5).

It was now obvious that what had appeared to be the northern side of the court was a separate feature, which abutted both the exposed rampart and the northern side of the cairn. It was also clear that the construction of this feature had disturbed the northern edge of the cairn.

This later feature was constructed, again, of stone and earth, and was 3.6m wide and 9.8m long within the area of excavation; however, it may continue eastward, outside the area under investigation.

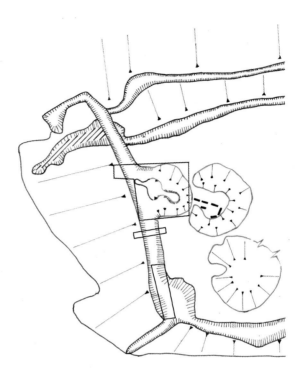

0   25m

Fig. 2—Plan of western end of limestone reef at Ballycarty, showing limits of excavation.

Pl. 5—The area of excavation following sod-stripping. The large stone in the centre left of the picture is part of the Phase 2 façade.

3. THE EXCAVATION

Pl. 6—The cairn from the north.

The excavation focused on two main areas, the cairn site and the rampart. Given the 49m length of the exposed rampart, it was decided to excavate five 2m-wide sections through this feature, one of which would be opened at the point where the rampart abutted the cairn on its southern side. A 2m-wide section would also be opened through the centre of the forecourt area and cairn.

THE CAIRN

The initial section through the cairn involved the removal of cairn material until the tops of larger structural stones were encountered. During work on this section two bronze ringed pins were recovered from directly under the topsoil—a spiral-ringed baluster-headed example, which was broken, and a very well-preserved stirrup-ringed crutch-headed example.

The cairn itself was revealed to be constructed of alternating layers of soil and stone. The soil layers were on average 0.22m thick and were all composed of a dark brown loamy soil. The stone used in the cairn was predominantly limestone with an average size of 0.15m by 0.15m by 0.2m. However, a large quantity of water-rolled red sandstone, which was very cleanly fractured and broken, was found scattered throughout the cairn, as were angular pieces of quartz and rock crystal. At this stage the southern half of the cairn was placed under investigation (Pl. 6).

THE SOUTHERN HALF OF THE CAIRN

The cairn material on the southern half of the site was again removed until larger structural stones were encountered. The tops of large stones, forming three concentric arcs, were visible on this side, while in the centre the tops of stones forming the side walls of a passage and D-shaped chamber could be seen. The area immediately above and inside the remains of the chamber and passage also contained a brown-black soil which was rich in charcoal (Pl. 7).

The remaining cairn material, which contained a number of stones larger than those in the main body of the cairn in the area between the D-shaped chamber and the inner of the three concentric arcs of stone, was removed to reveal a light brown redeposited boulder clay. This was very compact and contained flecks of charcoal, while the whole layer was very even and level with a maximum depth of 0.36m. Just inside the line of the inner arc of stone the clay was cut by four post-holes and a possible stone-socket.

Three of the post-holes were very shallow, with a maximum depth of 70mm, and are unlikely to have been capable of supporting any substantial post. They had diameters of between 110mm and 130mm. The best-preserved post-hole was the most easterly example. Like the others, it was filled with a dark grey soil which was removed to reveal the underlying limestone bedrock. Its basal fill produced a pair of bird claws. This post-hole measured 120mm by 140mm and was 270mm deep. The possible stone-socket was a large irregular depression close to the western extent of the inner arc of stone. It measured 200mm by 260mm and had a maximum depth of 190mm. Its shape indicated that whatever it had contained had been inserted at an angle (Pl. 8).

The redeposited boulder clay overlay the limestone bedrock and displayed evidence of burning along a line indicative of a complete inner ring of stone, now partially destroyed in the area of the D-shaped chamber and passage. There was, however, one small area of extensive burning on the northern side which extended beyond the conjectural line of a symmetrical inner ring. Two large stones resting on this area were probably the remains of the inner ring on this side of the site. The burning clearly ran under the stones so they were

Pl. 7—The D-shaped Phase 3 chamber and the tops of the structural stones of the Phase 1 chamber being exposed.

Pl. 8—Post-holes inside the south side of the Phase 1 chamber.

removed, but the burnt clay gave way to bedrock halfway under them.

The space between the inner and middle arcs of stone was tightly packed with earth and larger stones than elsewhere in the cairn, while the material between the middle and outer arcs was composed mainly of soil. Removal of this material revealed that the stones of the arcs rested on bedrock, with a redeposited boulder clay and stones used to pack around the bases. It also revealed that the gaps between the large boulders of the inner and middle arcs had been packed with smaller stones and some soil.

The soil around the stones between the middle and inner arcs was similar to the soil in the main body of the cairn for a depth of around 0.38m. Underlying this was up to 0.36m of the redeposited boulder clay, which produced three flint flakes. The soil between the outer and middle arcs was predominantly the redeposited boulder clay, which produced some animal bone and one water-rolled quartz pebble.

The inner arc measured 2.86m east–west and survived to a maximum height of 0.73m at its western extent. The middle arc survived to a maximum height of 1.2m, while the outer arc had a maximum height of only 0.56m.

At their western extent all three arcs changed from being constructed of large single stones to a rough walling using up to four rudimentary courses of large blocks. This walling varied in length from 1.3m for the inner arc to 2.1m for the outer arc, and a number of the stones were set with their long axes pointing into the tomb. The walling also had a definite inward batter, most visible in the inner arc. The ends of the arcs, where they curved toward the western side of the cairn, were terminated by two short cross-walls which spanned the gaps between them.

The short wall which terminated the inner and middle arcs was constructed of up to three courses of large stones and was 0.8m in length, while a 0.55m-long, sharp incurving of the outer arc closed the gap between the outer and middle arcs. This incurving piece of walling was of similar construction to the wall closing the inner and middle rings but was curved and set at right angles to the western end of the first wall. Both sections of walling were very similar to the walling at the western end of each arc, which they terminated.

Removal of collapse resting directly on redeposited boulder clay to the immediate north

Pl. 9—The Phase 1 passage blocked by the Phase 2 façade.

A

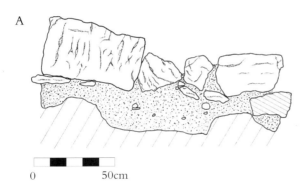

0   50cm

B

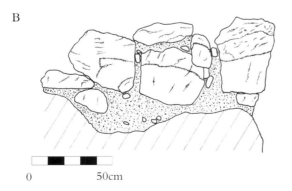

0   50cm

Fig. 3—Elevations of the side walls of the short Phase 1 passage: (A) north-facing, (B) south-facing.

of the wall terminating the inner and middle arcs revealed the presence of a second wall, again constructed of large irregular boulders.

These two walls formed the sides of a short, roughly built passage, 1.45m long, which contained a compact flooring of redeposited boulder clay, similar to that inside the inner arc. The passage was 0.74m wide at the entrance, increasing to 0.84m where it entered the inner arc. It had a maximum height of 0.6m, decreasing to 0.42m where the level of the bedrock was higher. At both sides of the entrance the walls rested on stones: the one on the southern side projected 0.23m into the passage, while that on the north side projected 0.12m. The distance between them was 0.39m, and they may have served as 'sill stones' (Pl. 9; Fig. 3).

It was noticeable that the arcs were higher and more substantial to the south-west, where in all three cases they consisted of at least two and up to four courses of large stones.

THE CHAMBER AND PASSAGE

There were large amounts of loose stone, indicative of collapse, in the immediate area of the D-shaped chamber, while the brown-black soil filling most of the extant chamber and passage contained charcoal and burnt stone.

This layer sealed the drystone-built chamber and overlay a loose grey-black deposit with evidence of burning, including charcoal and the largest quantity of cremated bone from the site. The layer also produced a perforated limestone bead. This deposit was found in both chamber and passage but ran under the stone setting of the chamber. The lowest levels of the chamber were filled with a redeposited boulder clay containing flecks of ash and charcoal and three fragments of cremated bone (Pl. 10).

In the passage an extant lintel, measuring 0.9m by 0.4m by 0.22m, was uncovered, and the portion of the passage from the lintel to the chamber had the same stratigraphy as the chamber, except that there was very little evidence for the lowest redeposited boulder clay.

Pl. 10—The D-shaped Phase 3 chamber and the Phase 2/3 passage.

A

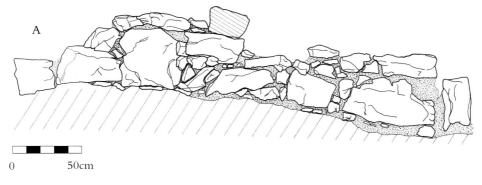

0   50cm

B

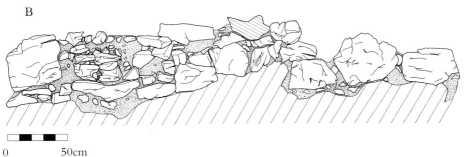

0   50cm

Fig. 4—Elevations of the side walls of the Phase 2/3 passage: (A) north-facing, (B) south-facing.

15

Pl. 11—The burnt layer inside the entrance to the Phase 3 passage.

Following the removal of numerous large stones, excavation in the outer portion of the passage showed that the basal layer here consisted of a very black, heavily burnt layer containing very high levels of wood charcoal and numerous lenses of red, white and grey ash. The stones in this area of the passage showed evidence of burning, as did some of the stones of the chamber (Pl. 11).

The passage has an unusual shape—doglegged at the entrance and then curving slightly all the way to the chamber. It is 3.13m long at the centre and narrows from a width of 0.84m at the entrance to 0.46m where it enters the chamber. The floor of the passage has been cut slightly into the bedrock; the floor level rises sharply toward the extant lintel and then drops into the chamber (Fig. 4).

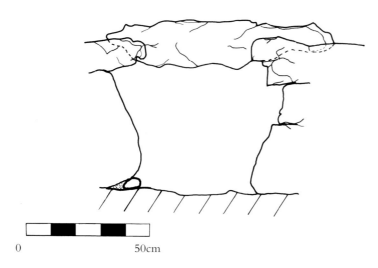

0   50cm

Fig. 5—Elevation of the Phase 2/3 passage at the extant lintel.

The extant lintel marks a change in the construction of the passage: from the lintel to the chamber it is constructed of slabs and boulders set on edge, while from the lintel to the entrance it is constructed of drystone walling. In its current position the lintel gives the passage, at this point, a height of 0.53m, but it appears to have slipped from on top of two stones immediately inside it, toward the chamber. These stones overhang the passage by 0.1m and 0.11m respectively, and when resting on them the lintel would have been 0.65m above the floor of the passage. The height of the lintel, coupled with the rising floor level, would have given the entrance to the passage a height of at least 0.9m (Fig. 5).

The D-shaped chamber is substantially collapsed, but up to three courses, 0.55m high, of drystone walling remain. The chamber is built into a rock-cut depression 0.44m below the level of the surrounding bedrock and measures 1.1m by 0.91m. However, the presence of a soil consistent with the general cairn material under the drystone settings indicates that it is a later addition.

THE FORECOURT

Excavations in this area commenced with the opening of a section through the interface between the rampart and the cairn on its southern side. Clearing down of this area revealed the presence of eight bowl-shaped depressions/pits, on average 0.26m in diameter and 0.18m deep, in the cairn material. These were filled with a mixture of soil and stone but produced no finds.

The removal of stone in this area revealed that the interface consisted of collapse from both cairn and rampart, the cairn stones being slightly smaller than those of the rampart. It also revealed that the rampart had curved sharply to the west to avoid the cairn. This section was then extended northward to encompass the forecourt area and the southern side of the court feature, denoted prior to excavation by the tops of four large stones. These were uncovered and proved to be four large slabs forming part of a curved façade constructed, in the main, of six large slabs and boulders, running from the southern side of the passage. The façade also utilised one narrow piece of bedrock outcrop close to the passage entrance, while the remaining portion, from this outcrop to the entrance, was constructed of drystone walling (Fig. 6).

The three concentric arcs of stone on the southern side of the cairn did not meet the façade, and the area between the arcs and the façade, on average 0.38m wide, was tightly packed with small stones and soil. The façade also ran in front of the short, roughly built passage, and one large boulder had been placed directly in front of its entrance.

Excavation of the area in front of the façade revealed that the stones rested on bedrock and that much cairn material had slipped from behind the façade. It also revealed the presence of two large slabs which had obviously fallen from on top of two of the extant façade stones. Given the combined height of these stones and the height of the tallest extant

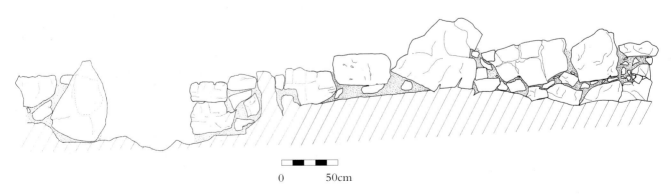

0   50cm

Fig. 6—Elevation of the curved Phase 2 façade.

Pl. 12—The U-shaped setting of stone used to contain the material which buttressed the rear of the Phase 2 façade where it overshot the cairn.

stone, the façade was originally at least 1.35m in height, decreasing as it moved away from the passage entrance.

Further excavation of this area also revealed the presence of a U-shaped stone setting, composed of ten medium-sized limestone blocks. The setting abutted the outer arc of stones at the west-north-west and curved around to end at the southern extent of the orthostatic façade. The setting was filled with smaller pieces of red sandstone, limestone and quartz fragments. Its opening faced north, toward the short, roughly built passage, and it measured 1.7m across and 1.1m in depth (Pl. 12).

Following the removal of all soil and earth from the forecourt area, five rock-cut pits were encountered. The largest (0.6m by 0.5m by 0.36m deep) was furthest from the cairn and is probably later. The other four were close together, measured between 0.3m and 0.4m in maximum length and were on average 0.28m deep. They were filled with a mixture of black soil, containing flecks of charcoal, and redeposited boulder clay. One of the pits contained a deposit of grey ash from which came three fragments of cremated bone (Pl. 13).

A THIRD PASSAGE

Complete excavation of the long passage and forecourt revealed the remains of a third passage entering the cairn from the western side.

It was now clear that the existing long passage was in fact an altered version of an earlier passage. The extant passage from the surviving lintel to the chamber was part of this earlier structure, while the southern side wall of the earlier passage from the lintel to the entrance was hidden by the later addition of a wedge-shaped section of

Pl. 13—One of the small rock-cut pits in the forecourt—this one produced burnt bone as well as the molar of a dog and a bone from a barn owl.

Pl. 14—The central depression on the surface of the cairn-like material on the north side of the forecourt; a D-sectioned post-hole was found directly under this depression.

drystone walling. The portion of the northern side wall from the lintel to the entrance was completely destroyed and replaced with a drystone wall.

The southern side of the original passage entrance was marked by the bedrock outcrop visible in the façade and utilised this natural outcrop for a length of 0.72m. This original passage wall appeared to be slab/boulder-built and 2.7m long, while the drystone walling seems to indicate later additions.

THE NORTH SIDE OF THE FORECOURT

A feature that originally seemed to form one side of the court could be seen, following soil-stripping, to be a separate structure. It was very straight-sided and could possibly have been an offshoot of the main rampart. However, it was more like a small mound of stone, piled in an area between two parallel planes of bedrock.

Cleaning down of the structure revealed a centrally placed subcircular depression, 0.55m by 0.5m by 0.29m deep. Its base was filled with loose stone and earth from the mound/bank; following removal of this material, the depression had a depth of 0.38m and came directly down onto a redeposited boulder clay which contained large amounts of charcoal (Pl. 14).

The excavation of this central area revealed a large post-hole and a much smaller stake-hole cut through the redeposited boulder clay at the base of the large depression. The post-hole was D-shaped and measured 0.22m by 0.15m by 0.17m deep. The circular stake-hole, 35mm east of the larger post-hole, had a diameter of 30mm and was 95mm deep. Both holes lay directly over a grike in the underlying bedrock, similar to the deepest of the post-holes in the centre of the cairn site.

The removal of stone from this mound/bank feature revealed that it was laid down very haphazardly and no coherent structure could be seen. It did, however, appear to be delimited on both its northern and southern sides by the planes of existing bedrock, which it followed. It became clear that this feature was responsible for disturbing part of the northern half of the cairn and that it was much later than the cairn (as evidenced by finds of iron slag). Some of the layers associated with this feature could be traced on top of the northern side of the cairn.

Excavation at the point where the feature abutted the north-western area of the cairn revealed a large rock-cut pit, 1.45m by 1.75m by 0.66m deep, which was completely filled with alternating layers of burnt soil and differently coloured ash. The pit also contained charcoal and large quantities of iron slag (Pl. 15; Fig. 7).

Pl. 15—A large rock-cut pit on the north side of the tomb. This pit was filled with burnt material and contained iron slag.

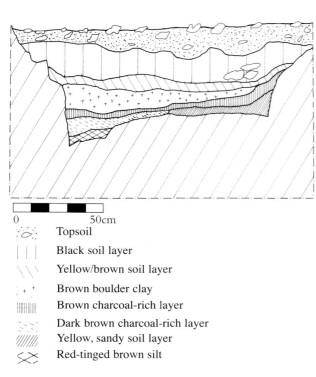

:ᴏ̇:	Topsoil
⏐⏐⏐	Black soil layer
\\\	Yellow/brown soil layer
₊₊	Brown boulder clay
⦀⦀⦀	Brown charcoal-rich layer
⁖⁖⁖	Dark brown charcoal-rich layer
⫽⫽⫽	Yellow, sandy soil layer
⨯⨯	Red-tinged brown silt

Fig. 7—Section through the fill of the rock-cut pit on the north side of the site.

THE NORTHERN HALF OF THE CAIRN

It was now obvious that the northern side of the site was greatly disturbed, and excavation of the cairn on this side revealed the extent of this disturbance. The layers extending from the structure to the west were traced over the northern side of the cairn, where they survived to a depth of 0.16m.

The cairn material was then removed. While the construction of the cairn was the same as on the southern side, the depth of cairn material was much less, on average only 0.23m. This was probably, in part, due to the disturbance of this side of the site and also to the fact that the underlying bedrock was higher than on the southern side. At one point on the northern side the bedrock had been deliberately chipped into a 'stepped' arrangement, giving it a superficial resemblance to a cairn and radically decreasing the amount of cairn material that would have to be used.

A large, 0.86m-deep, natural depression in the bedrock at the edge of the cairn site was found to have been completely filled with redeposited boulder clay, apparently during the construction of the cairn.

Owing to disturbance, only intermittent stretches of the outer two arcs of stone were uncovered on the northern side. However, it was now clear that originally these arcs had been three concentric rings of contiguous stones cut on the western side by the short, roughly built passage, the inner ring being destroyed on its northern side by the longer passage and the D-shaped chamber.

The remains of the outer two rings on this side were most complete where they curved towards the western side of the site and were constructed of large boulders; however, unlike the southern side of the site, the arcs on the northern side contained some quite small stones and also utilised existing bedrock outcrops. It was now also clear that there was a very sharp fall in the bedrock level from the northern to the southern side of the site, which gave the rings on the southern side a stepped profile.

The average distance between the rings was 0.55m and they increased in height as they approached either side of the short, roughly built passage.

THE RAMPART

The total length of the rampart exposed in the road-take area was 49m. As already noted, this stretch of rampart was not visible prior to sod-stripping but it did join with the extant rampart on the southern side of the spur and ran over the rampart on the northern side of the spur, where it continued downslope.

Five separate 2m-wide sections were opened across the rampart, with the most southerly two eventually being connected and those on either side of the cairn being incorporated into the general cairn excavation.

All across the site the rampart was very collapsed and on average 3m wide. Prior to excavation it appeared to be constructed of a mixture of limestone blocks and clay, randomly thrown together. The first section opened was centrally placed along the rampart and revealed that it was constructed on the crest of a natural rise in the level of the bedrock. The rampart was built directly on top of the bedrock and was laid down in alternating layers of earth and stone, with larger stones at the base, decreasing in size toward the top. There was no evidence for a foundation or trench, and this was repeated in all but the most northerly section (Pl. 16).

Pl. 16—The randomly constructed rampart built on a natural crest in the bedrock.

Pl. 17—The interior or eastern face of the wall in the southernmost rampart sections.

The second section was opened at the southern end of the rampart and initially appeared similar to the first section. However, following the excavation of material similar to that in the first section, an internally and externally faced wall was revealed in the centre of the structure.

The facing on the eastern side was the more finished, with three distinct courses of stone, while that on the west was very rough and uneven. The intervening space was filled with smaller stones and a dark brown clay to give a wall-like structure, on average 1m wide. The wall was built on the underlying bedrock and, in places, on a sterile boulder clay. The material that had surrounded this wall was laid down on the same mixture of bedrock and boulder clay as the wall itself; it showed no evidence of being collapse but rather appeared to have been deliberately built up around the wall (Pl. 17).

This section was extended northward for a further 2m and a similar structure was uncovered. The total exposed length of the wall was now 4m and it rose in height from the south toward the north. The western or exterior face of the wall was on average 0.08m higher than the eastern or interior face, the maximum height of the west face being 0.48m and that of the east face being 0.39m (Pl. 18).

Pl. 18—The exterior or western face of the rampart revealed in the southernmost sections.

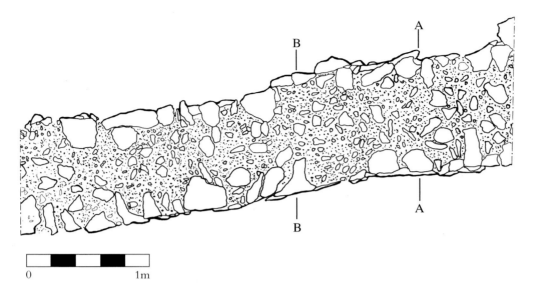

0   1m

Fig. 8—Plan of the faced wall found in the southernmost rampart sections, with sections A–A and B–B marked.

The third section was opened at the point where the rampart abutted the cairn and, while a line of stones which may have been the remains of a wall face were uncovered, it revealed a similar random structure to that of the first section, as did the fourth section. However, since a very straight line of stones could be seen on the ground surface between the fourth section and the extended second section, the intervening area was excavated.

This revealed that the double facing disappeared at the excavated extent of the second section but that a single wall face, on the western side, continued north for a further 1.32m

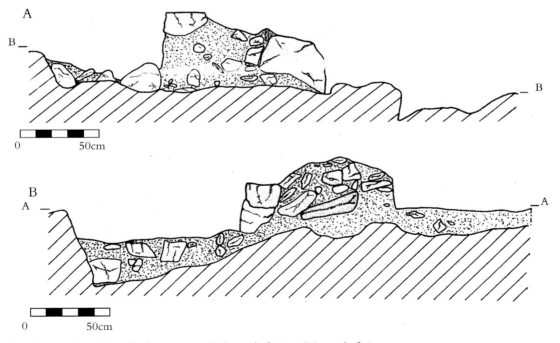

0   50cm

0   50cm

Fig. 9—Sections through the rampart: (A) south-facing, (B) north-facing.

23

before the structure assumed the random collapsed form of the other excavated areas. The east face of the rampart was very rough and did not look as if it were faced at any stage. This fourth section also revealed a dramatic increase in the width of the compact wall-like structure from the 1m of the double-faced section to a width of 2.3m where the single-faced section merged with the more random construction (Fig. 8).

The fifth and final section across the rampart was opened at a point in line with the northern side of the cairn and revealed the faced construction found in the second section at the opposite end of the rampart. Here the wall was more obvious; the volume of surrounding stone and earth material was much less and had the appearance of being collapse from the wall itself rather than material deliberately piled around the wall. There was also evidence of a natural buildup of soil amidst and under the collapse (Fig. 9).

The facing of the western side of the wall here was better than that at the southern end of the rampart, while that on the eastern side was less well defined owing to the use of smaller stones. The wall was of similar width, on average 0.85m, to that in the second section, but only one true course of stone was visible (average height 0.32m). However, unlike the similar wall at the other end of the site, the wall in this section was cut into an orange/brown boulder clay with stone inclusions rather than built directly on the underlying bedrock (Fig. 10).

Prior to the excavation there was a noticeable area, clear of stone and with a differing soil colour, immediately inside (east of) the rampart. The area was 1.65m wide and stretched from the southern extent of the rampart to the south side of the cairn. However, when the relevant sections were extended through this area no evidence for an infilled ditch or other feature was forthcoming. It may be that this area was cleared to serve as a walkway or access line inside the rampart.

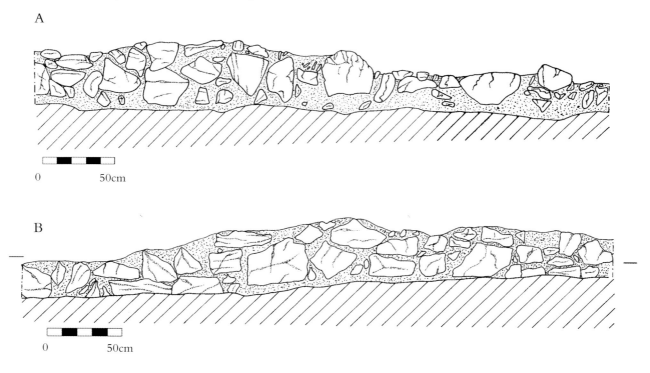

A

0   50cm

B

0   50cm

Fig. 10—Elevations of walled rampart in southernmost sections: (A) west face, (B) east face.

4. THE FINDS

(The lithic assemblage from the site is described and discussed separately in Appendix 1.)

STONE PENDANT

96E138:55 An irregularly shaped piece of water-rolled limestone with a domed profile. It is rounded but has a flat back and is narrower and thicker at one end. The rounded or front face is covered in small deep pock-marks, caused by the action of marine sponges on the stone. The stone is transversely perforated through its wider and thinner end. The perforation is circular in section, 2mm in diameter and 3mm deep. This transverse perforation allows the stone to hang straight with the domed face toward the front. The bead measures 16mm by 9mm by 7mm and was found in the fill of the Phase 2/3 chamber (Pl. 19; Fig. 11).

SHARPENING OR RUBBING STONES

96E138:1 Subrectangular piece of red sandstone, 105mm long, 47mm wide and 32mm thick. It tapers toward one end, and all faces, except the broader end, show evidence of picking, but no scorings can be seen on the surface. It was found immediately under the topsoil in the forecourt.

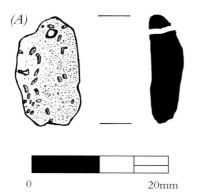

(A)

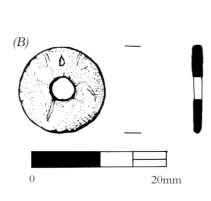

(B)

0   20mm

0   5cm

Fig. 11—(A) Stone pendant; (B) antler disc bead.   *Pl. 19—The limestone pendant (no. 55).*

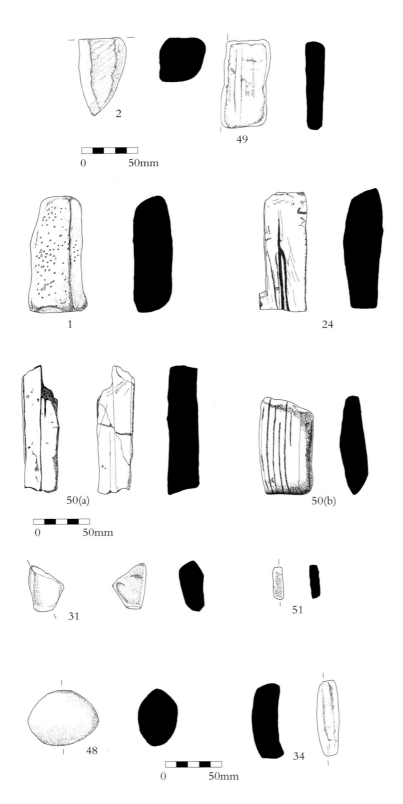

Fig. 12—A selection of rubbing stones, a water-rolled quartz 'ball' and a portion of a possible lignite disc.

96E138:2 An almost round-sectioned, irregularly shaped piece of red sandstone, 84mm long, 62mm wide and 50mm thick. It is perfectly flat and smooth at one end, probably owing to having been deliberately cut, and tapers slightly toward the other end. It has one narrow, flat facet which bears a number of shallow, diagonal scorings. This stone was, again, found under the topsoil in the forecourt.

96E138:24 A rectangular-sectioned piece of green sandstone, 105mm long, 38mm wide and 24mm thick. It is flat and smooth at one end, where it appears to have been broken, while the other end is rough and uneven. Both sides and one face are smooth and flat, the other face being quite rough. The smooth face bears three deep scorings and some other minor scratches. The central scoring is 3.5mm deep and 85mm long to the broken end of the stone. The scorings appear to have been made by an edged or pointed implement. This stone was found near the northern edge of the cairn in a very disturbed area (Pl. 20; Fig. 12).

Pl. 20—Rubbing stones: (top) nos 50 and 34; (bottom) nos 24 and 49.

96E138:34 An almost crescentic piece of dark grey limestone, 66mm long, 24mm wide and 19mm thick. It is very smooth and has a distinct polish, as if from much use. Both sides have a light brown colour and a different texture to the rest. This discolouration may result from rubbing hides or some other such use. One of the sides bears two 1mm–deep grooves running the length of the stone and over one end. The stone was found within the cairn material on the north side of the site.

96E138:49 A rectangular piece of red sandstone, 82mm long, 37mm wide and 19mm thick. Both faces of the stone are quite flat, while the sides and ends are rough and uneven. The two faces bear a number of very shallow scorings. The stone was found immediately under the topsoil on the northern side of the cairn and may have been a pin–sharpener.

96E138:50 A subrectangular piece of green sandstone, 90mm long, 60mm wide and 23mm thick. Both faces and sides of the stone are quite smooth, while both ends are very rough and uneven. Both faces bear a number of shallow scorings which may be evidence of use as a sharpening stone. The stone was found just outside the kerb on the southern side of the cairn.

WATER-ROLLED STONE

96E138:48 Very smooth, subspherical piece of water-rolled quartz measuring 60mm by 53mm. It bears no evidence of working and was found inside the line of the Phase 1 chamber on the eastern side.

Pl. 21—(top) Water-rolled quartz pebbles (L–R: nos 58, 64 and 57); (bottom) water-rolled sandstone and quartz pebbles (L–R: nos 60, 59 and 48).

96E138:57 An irregularly shaped piece of very white, smooth, water-rolled quartz, again with no evidence of working. It was found in the redeposited boulder clay inside the Phase 1 chamber on the southern side of the site.

96E138:58 A subspherical piece of water-rolled quartz measuring 71mm by 63mm. This stone is not as flawlessly smooth as the other two pieces, and a number of fractures and cracks are visible on its surface. One area exhibits very clear evidence of burning. The stone was found close to no. 57 above (Pl. 21).

96E138:59 An almost spherical piece of red sandstone measuring 36mm by 34mm. It bears some evidence of picking but would seem to have been mainly fashioned through water action. The stone is very brittle and bears evidence of burning. It was found inside the Phase 1 chamber, close to the structural stones on the southern side.

96E138:60 Subspherical piece of green sandstone measuring 36mm by 31mm. It is quite smooth and bears no evidence of working. It was found close to no. 59 above, and displays similar evidence of having been subjected to fire.

96E138:62 An irregularly shaped piece of water-rolled red sandstone measuring 50mm by 40mm. It was found within the Phase 1 chamber, near its eastern side, and bears clear evidence of having been subjected to heat, one side being bleached almost white.

96E138:63 A quartered piece of quartz conglomerate rock from what was originally a subspherical water-rolled stone. The extant piece measures 50mm by 30mm by 30mm. The smoothness of the broken sides and the evidence for burning on its curved exterior suggest that it shattered during subjection to intense heat. This piece was found in the fill of the Phase 2/3 passage, close to the chamber.

96E138:64 A small subspherical piece of water-rolled quartz measuring 39mm by 39mm. It was found in a disturbed context on the northern side of the cairn.

96E138:65 One half of what was originally a subspherical water-rolled piece of red sandstone. The extant half measures 57mm by 41mm and was subjected to intense heat, which may well have been the cause of its breaking. It was found in the fill of the Phase 2/3 chamber.

MISCELLANEOUS STONE

96E138:21 A & B Two large red sandstone fragments found side by side on the surface of the cairn, beneath the topsoil, directly over the Phase 1 passage. Fragment A is subrectangular with one curved end, and is 245mm long, 118mm wide and 61mm thick. One face of the stone and the curved end have been carefully worked and dressed. Fragment B is triangular, though the base of the triangle is, again, curved. It is 204mm long, 181mm wide and 61mm thick. Again one face and the curved section have been worked and dressed. The two fragments fit neatly together to give a combined triangular fragment measuring 310mm by 245mm by 61mm. The pieces would appear to be fragments of a millstone, which would originally have had a diameter of between 0.75m and 0.8m (Pl. 22).

96E138:31 A subspherical piece of limestone with one slightly concave surface. It has the look and texture of marble owing to polishing or extensive use. It measures 23mm by 19mm and has a brown discolouration on the concave surface, as if it had been used to rub leather or hide. It was found in one of the shallow post-holes inside the southern side of the Phase 1 chamber.

96E138:36 An ovoid piece of limestone which, like no. 31, has the look and texture of marble. It measures 24mm by 19mm and has thin veins of a ferrous material running around its exterior. It was found close to no. 31 above.

96E138:43 A large, saddle-shaped red sandstone fragment measuring 450mm by 280mm by 170mm. It is generally smooth and appears to have broken along the line of a centrally placed circular boring, 37.5mm in diameter and 19mm deep. The stone has one damaged area, 70mm from this boring, which includes two further subcircular depressions. These are 30mm in diameter and 10mm deep and appear to be the result of blows with a heavy object. The stone was found at the western limit of the excavation and the missing portion may lie outside this line. It was partly resting in the basal boulder clay, directly under the topsoil, outside the rampart and may have functioned as an anvil (Pl. 23).

Pl. 22—Fragmentary millstone (no. 21 A and B).

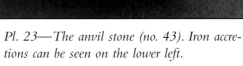

Pl. 23—The anvil stone (no. 43). Iron accretions can be seen on the lower left.

Pl. 24—*Red sandstone disc (no. 61). This object is clearly worked and was subjected to intense heat.*

Pl. 25—*Antler disc bead (no. 26).*

96E138:61 Circular disc of red sandstone, 49mm in diameter and 14mm thick. The stone has been chipped but would appear to originally have had a concave edge. Both faces are fairly flat and bear definite traces of working. The stone is dry and brittle, which suggests that it has been subjected to fire. It was found inside the line of the Phase 1 chamber close to no. 62 above (Pl. 24).

96E138:69 Very smooth, rounded pebble with iron adhesions, found at the interface between the cairn and the rampart.

ANTLER DISC BEAD

96E138:26 This flat, circular disc of antler was found in remnants of the cairn material on the very disturbed northern side of the cairn. It has a diameter of 16mm, is 1.5–2mm thick and has a central perforation 6mm in diameter. All surfaces of the bead show scoring and evidence of wear (Pl. 25; Fig. 11).

POTTERY

96E138:23 A small piece of a possible crucible-like material, 16mm by 15mm by 9mm thick, with traces of what may be a red glaze on its outer surface. It was found in a stony deposit underneath the rampart masonry in the most northerly rampart section.

96E138:54 A possible rim fragment of a ceramic crucible, 26mm by 22mm by 8mm thick, with a small patch of what may be a red glaze on its outer surface. This piece was found in the same place as no. 23 above.

96E138:46 A small sherd of highly fired medieval pottery, 18mm by 13mm by 6mm thick, which was recovered from the very disturbed boulder clay on the north side of the cairn.

RINGED PINS

96E138:2 A bronze ringed pin found immediately under the topsoil, resting on the cairn material, close to the centre of the cairn. It was intact and in a remarkably good state of preservation.

The shank of the pin is 69mm in overall length and curves slightly from the head to the point. The head, of 'crutch' form and set at a slight angle to the shank, is square-sectioned and measures 8mm in length, 4mm in width and 3mm in height. The sockets on either side of the head are circular and 2.5mm in diameter (Pl. 26).

The ring is of 'stirrup' form and is D-shaped in section. It is attached to the head by small tenons inserted into the sockets on either side of the head. The ring itself measures 8mm from side to side and 12mm from the surface of the crutch head to the top.

The overall length of the pin, with ring extended, is 80mm (Fig. 13).

96E138:13 This pin, like that described above, was found resting on the upper surface of the cairn, directly beneath the topsoil, in the eastern quadrant of the site. The shank and ring were each broken into two pieces and all four fragments were heavily patinated and brittle.

The shank of the pin is 87mm in overall length and bends sharply 75mm from its top. It tapers gently from the head to the point.

The head is of typical 'baluster' form—it is square-sectioned and has central lozenge-shaped panels delimited above and below by collars or fillets. There is some damage to the head, particularly to the lozenge-shaped panels, which

Pl. 26—The ringed pins after conservation— crutch-headed (no. 2) on the left, baluster-headed (no. 13) on the right.

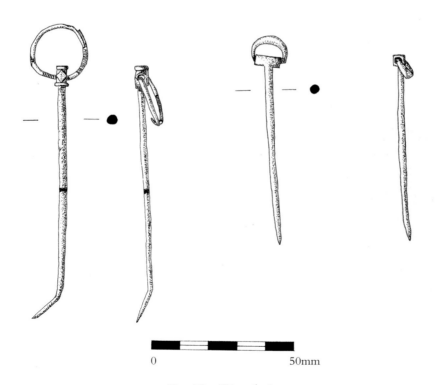

0   50mm

Fig. 13—Ringed pins.

are chipped. The perforation to the head is circular in section and 3mm in diameter. The head measures 7.5mm in maximum length and 4mm in maximum width.

The ring is of the 'spiral' type, consisting of a strip of wire threaded through the head and wound in spiral fashion. Part of the ring would appear to be missing, as there is evidence of a second break at one of the surviving ends and the ring is not long enough to terminate at either side of the head, as in classic examples. The wire ring is circular in section and 1.8mm thick. It was originally 18mm in diameter and bears characteristic milling or ribbing on alternate arcs of its surface.

The overall length of the pin, with ring extended, is 110mm.

CLAY PIPES

96E138:5 An almost complete clay pipe bowl from topsoil directly on top of the rampart. One fragment is broken from the rim on the side nearest the stem. The bowl is widest at its centre and tapers toward top and bottom. It is 39mm long and 19mm wide (at mid-point). The diameter of the bowl opening is 14mm. The attached stem is 20mm long and 9mm in diameter and has a 3mm-diameter perforation.

96E138:22 Part of a clay pipe bowl from directly under topsoil outside the rampart. The fragment is 35mm long, 27mm wide and 6mm thick at the bowl rim. There is a 3mm-wide band of impressed decoration, composed of spaced parallel lines, just below the rim.

96E138:27 Part of a clay pipe stem from topsoil overlying the rampart in the most northerly excavated section. The piece is 30mm long and 6mm in diameter with a 2.5mm-diameter perforation.

96E138:39 Part of a clay pipe stem from topsoil above the rampart. The piece is 55mm long and 7mm in diameter and has a 2.5mm-diameter perforation.

5. CONSTRUCTION AND INTERPRETATION

There is little doubt, on the basis of stratigraphy and construction style, that the megalithic structure exhibits three main phases of activity and that a passage relating to each phase survives in the remains of the site (Fig. 14).

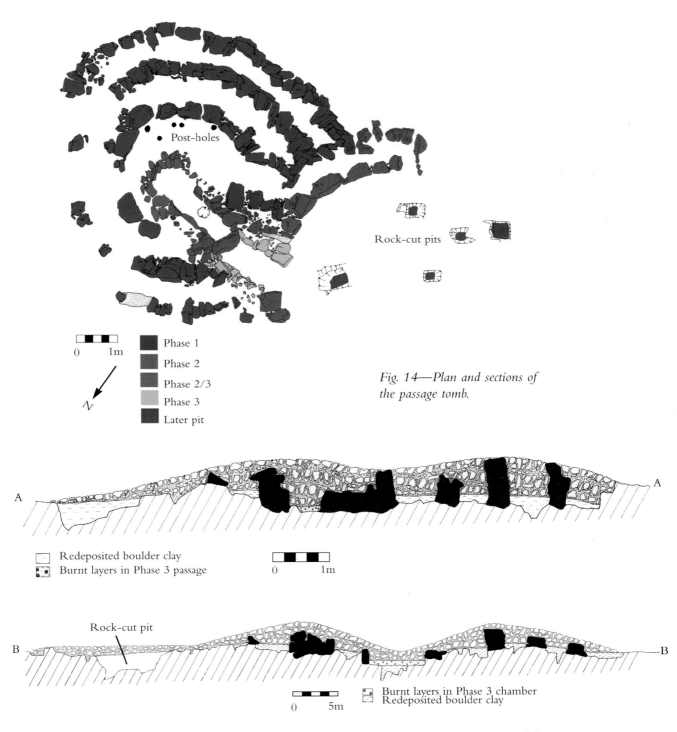

Post-holes

Rock-cut pits

0   1m

Phase 1
Phase 2
Phase 2/3
Phase 3
Later pit

N

Fig. 14—Plan and sections of the passage tomb.

A   A

☐ Redeposited boulder clay
▨ Burnt layers in Phase 3 passage

0   1m

Rock-cut pit

B   B

▨ Burnt layers in Phase 3 chamber
☐ Redeposited boulder clay

0   5m

33

Pl. 27—Aerial shot of the tomb from the south; the probable line of the Phase 1 chamber can be seen as a discolouration of the bedrock.

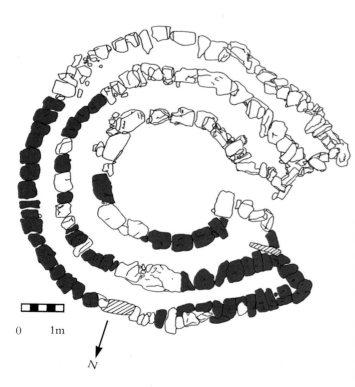

Fig. 15—Suggested reconstruction of the Phase 1 monument (conjectural stones shaded).

PHASE 1

Construction

Phase 1 saw the deliberate clearing of the site, the cutting away of portions of the bedrock, and the construction of the three concentric rings of contiguous stones, the outer serving as a kerb, cut by the short passage on their western side. The average internal diameters of the stone rings, from inner to outer, were 2.86m, 3.85m and 5.28m respectively (Pl. 27; Fig. 15).

The extant remains of the stone rings are composed of large limestone boulders and slabs, average dimensions 0.8m by 0.6m x 0.5m. Eight single-course boulders survive in the inner ring, sixteen in the middle ring, including the largest stone on the site, and 23 in the kerb.

However, some drystone walling is extant in all three rings at their western extent, from a point level with the centre of the inner ring. In the middle ring this walling is composed of three courses to a height of 0.8m. In the inner ring two courses remain to a height of 0.65m, while the outer ring or kerb has three courses remaining to a height of 0.75m. The use of a number of smaller stones rather than one large stone, sometimes in rudimentary courses, is also evident in other areas of the middle ring and the kerb.

The side walls of the short passage terminate and close off the gap between the inner and middle rings of boulders, while on the southern side of the tomb the gap between the middle ring and the kerb is closed by a sharp incurving of the kerb. On the northern side the incurving kerb has been destroyed by the insertion of the later passage.

However, if the destroyed portion of the kerb was similar to the surviving example on the southern side, this Phase 1 monument would have had a very roughly built curved façade, giving an almost funnel-shaped entrance to the passage.

The area inside the inner ring, which remains to a maximum height of 0.73m, had an average diameter of 2.86m. Given the fact that it seems to have had a prepared floor of redeposited boulder clay and displayed evidence of burning, there is little doubt that it was the focus of the Phase 1 monument and functioned as a chamber, entered through the short passage.

The extant remains of the chamber and the probable line of the removed blocks, as indicated by the burnt floor area, suggest that the chamber was most probably subcircular, although the small area of burning which extended from the conjectural line of the chamber on the north side may be evidence of a recess or antechamber, now destroyed.

The four post-holes found on the south side of the chamber may have supported one side of some form of wooden roof or mortuary structure, while any post-holes on the north side or centrally placed would have been destroyed by the later chamber and passage. However, three of the surviving post-holes are very shallow and, given that they occur directly above clints in the underlying bedrock, may have been failed attempts to drive a single post, which was successfully driven into a grike on the fourth attempt.

The large irregular depression at the western extent of the inner ring is almost certainly related to this period of activity and may have held a stone or large timber post, inserted at an angle, which supported a structure inside the chamber.

The 1.45m-long passage, which enters the chamber from the west, was floored with a redeposited boulder clay similar to that found inside the chamber. The sides of the passage remain to an average height of 0.54m and are constructed of large, irregularly shaped limestone blocks with average dimensions of 0.48m by 0.38m by 0.26m.

The south side wall is composed of two substantial blocks at either end with two smaller blocks between them. The northern side wall is composed of three blocks which increase in size from entrance to chamber. Indeed, both walls increase in height from entrance to chamber.

The passage contained a considerable number of collapsed large stones, probably displaced from the side walls. It was probably lintelled, though no possible example was recovered.

Interpretation

Prior to the construction of the Ballycarty tomb all the overlying boulder clay was stripped off, as evidenced by the lack of this basal layer in the forecourt area and the presence of secondary deposits within the redeposited clay. This stripping of the site would have facilitated the partial levelling of the bedrock and the placing of the structural stones directly onto the bedrock, rather than on or through the overlying boulder clay. This would probably have enabled the stones to be stabilised and may even have influenced the choice of the exact spot on which the tomb was built.

However, following the construction of the tomb the boulder clay was redeposited inside the monument to level off the interior and form a 'floor' within the passage and chamber.

It was also used as part of the packing between the structural stone settings. This redeposited boulder clay shows evidence of having been burnt, extensively in some areas, inside the chamber.

The cairn at Ballycarty was subcircular, in keeping with the usual form, and was surrounded by a stone kerb. However, whereas in many Irish examples the kerb is formed by a contiguous line of slabs or boulders, the Ballycarty kerb, in places, took the form of drystone walling, in particular on either side of the façade, which in Phase 1 was also constructed using a very rough drystone-walling technique.

The entranceway to the Phase 1 monument was formed by a sharp incurving of the kerb, creating a shallow, almost funnel-shaped entrance. The way in which the walls of the block-built passage articulate with the incurving kerb makes it highly unlikely that they could ever have been any higher than they are today without a corresponding increase in the height of the kerb.

This, in effect, means that the kerb on either side of the entrance and around part of the sides of the cairn, as shown by the extant walling, was built up as a drystone wall both to retain the cairn and to provide a monumental façade for the front of the tomb.

It is also clear, given the natural slope of the bedrock, that this walling would have been more substantial to the south of the entrance than to the north.

The Phase 1 chamber appears to have been constructed of large limestone blocks and drystone walling. The final height of the chamber would have been dictated by the fact that the structural stones are not set in sockets but rest directly on the underlying bedrock, with some clay and smaller stones used to fill the gaps in between and to stabilise them.

The tight packing of large stones between the chamber and the middle ring of orthostats would have added structural stability and appears to have formed a stone core to the monument, with the middle ring acting as a delimiting kerb. Interestingly, the middle ring is composed of some of the largest stones on the site, which would indicate that it was intended to act as a substantial buttress for the chamber. This would probably have enabled the chamber to attain a respectable height of 1.5m or more without collapsing.

The actual roofing of the Phase 1 chamber is problematic, as no stones large enough to have served as lintels or capstones were recovered, and it does, initially, seem unlikely that the chamber, buttressed by the core and its delimiting kerb, could have supported a fully corbelled roof and the overburden of cairn material.

However, the beginnings of a corbelled structure can be seen in the extant portion of the chamber closest to the south wall of the entrance passage and at the same point in the remains of the middle ring and kerb. In fact the construction of all three elements—chamber, middle ring and kerb—changes from the use of single large stones to courses of walling, from a point level with the centre of the chamber to the entrance passage.

In all three cases the walling has a distinct curvature, and the upper course of the extant wall in the kerb and middle ring is laid with the long axes of the stones pointing in towards the chamber. This would have meant that the upper levels of the middle ring and kerb would have locked into the core and packing inside them. Indeed, the stone packing between each of these three concentric elements of the site was composed of very large stones and, owing to the natural fall of the bedrock, remained up to a depth of 1.3m.

The natural fall of the bedrock toward this area of the site may offer some reason for this change in construction (the distinct inward curvature of the walling and the provision of such heavy packing). However, the extant portion of the middle ring, closest to the Phase 1 passage, on the very disturbed northern half of the site is also constructed of walling with a distinct curvature. This indicates that the front or westerly half of the site was being reinforced and balanced inward to counteract the outward pressure of a considerable weight, the thrust of which was toward the front of the tomb.

The possibility of a stone roof therefore cannot be discounted. However, the presence of post-holes inside the chamber offers the alternative of a wooden roof, formed by timbers resting on the upper surface of the chamber walls and supported by the internal posts.

Post-holes were found only on the southern side of the Phase 1 chamber, but any similar holes on the northern side or evidence for a central post would have been destroyed by the subsequent alterations to the site. It is even possible that the rock-cut subcircular depression which acts as the Phase 2/3 chamber may originally have been the socket for a large wooden upright, which would have been held in place by stone packing. The socket need not have been as wide as it is now—1.1m by 0.91m—and may have been chosen as the site for the smaller Phase 2 chamber owing to the ease with which it could be extended.

Indeed, the provision of even a wooden roof may have necessitated the construction changes and reinforcement of the western half of the tomb.

The only other features which may relate to the primary phase of use of the monument are the five rock-cut pits found outside the entrance to the tomb. One of these, the most westerly example, was cut through the boulder clay which overlay the bedrock everywhere except in the area of the tomb. This fact, coupled with the association of the anvil stone (96E138:43) with the pit, indicates that this pit is quite late.

The other pits were in an area where there was no boulder clay and which was most probably cleared of this material at the time of the construction of the primary monument. Yet this does not prove whether they were built at this time or are related to one of the two succeeding periods of activity at the site.

Given the limited stratigraphy in the area of the pits and the uniformity of their fill—burnt soil, ash, stone and some bone fragments—it is impossible to assign them with certainty to any of the three phases of activity. However, the failure to redeposit any boulder clay in this area following the construction of the Phase 1 monument may indicate that this area was to be kept clear for burial rituals, as indicated by the pits, and this may point to an original association with the Phase 1 tomb.

The entrance passage to the Phase 1 chamber is quite short at 1.45m. The Phase 1 monument had maximum dimensions of 7.34m east–west and 7.14m north–south.

PHASE 2

Construction
This phase saw the construction of the curved façade on the western side of the site and the insertion of a secondary passage and chamber (Fig. 16).

The façade on the southern side of the Phase 2 passage was originally constructed of six large boulders and slabs, ranging in size from 0.58m by 0.52m by 0.35m to 0.8m by 0.66m by 0.42m, and was terminated at its northern end by a piece of bedrock outcrop, 0.5m high and 0.35m wide at the base. Only two *in situ* and one collapsed stone (replaced during conservation works) of the façade on the north side of the long passage remain.

This façade seems to have followed the curve of the Phase 1 façade but it was not set tightly against the existing structure.

Eccentrically placed through this façade was a slab-built passage, orientated west-north-west/east-south-east, utilising the existing bedrock outcrop, which terminates one side of the façade, for a length of 0.74m. This passage was later altered in Phase 3, and only the southern side wall and a 1.68m-long stretch of the northern side wall (the portion nearest to the chamber) remain.

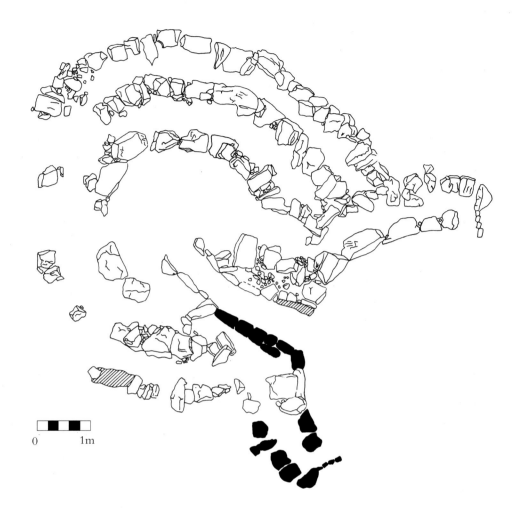

Fig. 16—Suggested reconstruction of the Phase 2 monument (conjectural stones shaded).

Apart from the 0.74m-long stretch of bedrock outcrop, the southern side of this passage was composed of four limestone slabs, on average 0.5m high and 0.55m wide. The extant portion of the northern side wall is composed of three stones of similar dimensions.

This 3.14m-long passage was probably roofed using lintels, similar to the extant example, which rested on large, heavy, overhanging slabs, again similar to the extant examples, which overhang the passage by 0.15m and 0.14m respectively and measure 0.6m by 0.25m by 0.2m and 0.55m by 0.4m by 0.12m.

The passage led to the area of the D-shaped drystone-built chamber, which was constructed in a deliberately executed subrectangular cut, 0.46m deep, in the limestone bedrock. The extant remains consist of four courses of drystone walling, but the chamber was probably corbelled to its full height or to a point where it could easily be roofed with a single lintel, a suggestion substantiated by the amount of collapse found in and around the chamber.

However, the possibility that the drystone walling of the chamber is a later Phase 3 addition cannot be discounted. Perhaps the Phase 2 chamber was constructed of orthostats lining the cut in the bedrock, or the Phase 2 passage utilised the primary chamber. The Phase 2 passage could also have been undifferentiated or could have used a now completely destroyed chamber. There is no real evidence as to what form the inner end of the Phase 2 passage took, and it can only be said that the reused portion of this passage led into the D-shaped drystone-built chamber in Phase 3.

The U-shaped setting of stones which curves from the western extent of the Phase 2 façade back to abut the kerb also relates to this phase of activity at the site. The Phase 2 monument had maximum dimensions of 8.34m east–west and 7.34m north–south.

Interpretation

Given the extensive damage to the northern half of the Phase 1 monument, it is reasonable to assume that the Phase 2 alterations to the site were effected following entry to the body of the cairn from this area.

The bedrock was cut and levelled in preparation for a new chamber and passage, while those features of the primary monument which were an obstruction were removed. It may even have been the collapse of the primary chamber that prompted the construction of this secondary passage and chamber.

However, the length and orientation of the passage appear to have been dictated by the reuse of a long slab-like outcrop of bedrock which originally formed part of the middle ring and façade of the Phase 1 monument. This in effect made the passage too long and badly aligned to be encompassed by the original façade and cairn.

The cairn had therefore to be extended slightly on its western side and completed with a substantial façade. This façade is an unusual feature: unlike the curved Phase 1 façade, which was formed by a very sharp incurving of the delimiting kerb, the Phase 2 façade was unconnected to any feature of the monument except the Phase 2 passage. It effectively sealed the Phase 1 passage, and the extension of the cairn behind it would have necessitated the deliberate filling of the primary passage, probably with material from the side walls of the passage.

It would seem likely, given their number and size, that this façade was constructed using large stones removed from the northern side of the Phase 1 chamber during the secondary alterations to the interior of the monument. The finding of a number of large slab-like stones directly in front of the façade also indicates that this Phase 2 façade was composed, at least in some areas, of two courses of large slabs and reached an original height of at least 1.3m.

The remains of this façade on the south side of the passage actually run beyond the side of the cairn, and presumably a similar arrangement existed on the more disturbed northern side. Indeed, the U-shaped setting which curves back from the end of the façade to the kerb on the southern side of the site did consist of more than one course of stones and contained numerous smaller stones. This packing was similar to that between the Phase 1 and Phase 2 façades, and was obviously used to buttress and support the section of the Phase 2 façade which overran the cairn.

The Phase 2 façade seems to have been partly an attempt to replicate the shape and form of the entrance to the Phase 1 monument, and partly, on a more functional level, a retaining feature for the extended cairn. If this was the case, then the experiment was only a partial success, as the west-north-west/east-south-east orientation of the Phase 2 passage meant that it was eccentrically placed to the secondary façade and the symmetry of the Phase 1 monument was lost.

The extension of the western side of the cairn and the construction of the façade increased the maximum dimension of the site to 8.34m east–west, while the north–south measurement of 7.34m remained the same.

PHASE 3

Construction

This phase saw the realignment of the front (north-westerly) portion of the Phase 2 passage and, possibly, the construction of the drystone-built chamber into which the realigned passage leads.

The realignment of the passage was achieved through the destruction of the outer portion of the slab-built Phase 2 northern side wall and the construction of a new drystone wall, while on the southern side a wedge-shaped section of drystone walling was added to the existing passage.

The new wall on the northern side of the passage remains to a height of 0.6m and a length of 0.88m, and consists of four courses of relatively small stones. The wedge-shaped section of walling added to the southern side of the Phase 2 passage is 0.6m high, 2.11m long and 0.62m wide at the entrance. It is constructed of large flat blocks in two main courses.

The point of realignment is marked by the extant lintel—that part of the passage north-west of the lintel was realigned, and that south-east of the lintel is the original Phase 2 passage. This change is also evidenced by the fact that the Phase 3 additions are constructed of drystone walling, while the Phase 2 passage is orthostatic.

This realignment pushed the passage entrance 0.61m further north, close to the probable northern extent of the Phase 2 façade.

Interpretation

During this phase the only alterations undertaken were the realignment of the outer portion of the Phase 2 passage, through the use of drystone walling, and probably the construction of the D-shaped drystone-built chamber. These alterations may have been undertaken to reuse the site for burial and to realign the entrance on a specific point.

However, the possibility that these alterations to the passage and the construction of the drystone-built chamber were undertaken to allow the reuse of the Phase 2 structure at a much later date, for a purpose other than burial, cannot be discounted. It would also appear that the mound of stone which formed a bank-like feature on the north side of the forecourt area is composed of material removed from the cairn, at a time when it was no longer being used as a place of burial. This may have taken place during Phase 3, when the Phase 2 monument was being altered for a use which did not necessitate a covering cairn.

Indeed, the extant Phase 3 passage and chamber bear comparison with corn-drying kilns excavated at Emlagh, Co. Kerry (Ó Ríordáin 1941, 98–9), and Ballynareha, Co. Tipperary (Gowen 1988, 158–62), and it may be that the realignment was necessary to improve the draught in a passage that was to be reused as a flue. A smaller, more compact chamber may also have been more suitable for the purpose of corn-drying, and, given the similarity between the small-scale drystone walling of the extant chamber and the passage alterations, as opposed to the large-scale block walling of the Phase 1 passage, these features are probably coeval.

The lack of substantial amounts of grain from the site and fire damage to the stones of the passage, as well as the finds of cremated bone and the perforated stone pendant/bead from the chamber, would argue against this suggestion, as would the relatively early radiocarbon date (cal. 96 BC–AD 75) from the substantial deposits of wood charcoal in the outer portion of the passage.

Therefore, a reuse as a place of burial, in the passage tomb tradition, would appear more likely for the Phase 3 monument.

THE CAIRN

The cairn was definitely in place during the second phase of activity, as the wedge-shaped section of walling used to realign the southern side of the passage in Phase 3 rests on the dark brown soil which formed around 40% of the cairn material. This soil could have slipped into the Phase 2 passage when the cairn was erected or, more probably, when the cairn was opened to perform the Phase 3 alterations.

The question of whether or not the Phase 1 structure was covered by a cairn is not so easily answered. Several pieces of evidence seem to indicate that there was a cairn in Phase 1 of the site—the most westerly-facing portions of all three stone rings on the southern side of the cairn are built of at least two, and in the case of the outer ring three, courses of large boulders, where there is the sharpest drop in the bedrock level; the difference between the general cairn material and that used to pack the gap between the Phase 2 façade and the Phase 1 structure; and the fact that the stones of the orthostatic façade rest on a soil consistent with that of the cairn material.

The most conclusive evidence comes from the portion of the Phase 2 passage nearest the chamber, where the orthostats forming the passage rest on a dark brown soil similar to the cairn material. This indicates that a cairn was in place prior to the construction of the Phase 2 passage.

Given this evidence and the lack of differentiation in the cairn, one would have to assume that the Phase 1 site, including the central area, was covered by a cairn, with the outer ring acting as a kerb and the middle ring stabilising the cairn.

6. DISCUSSION

There seems little doubt that the megalithic tomb at Ballycarty is a multi-period passage tomb. Many aspects of its construction, design and use find parallels amongst other Irish tombs of this type, yet it also exhibits some unusual features. It is clear that the limestone reef retained an attraction and possibly a ritual significance for people long after the period of the tomb's use.

Pl. 28—The large cairn on Knockawaddra Mountain. The base/kerb of the cairn can be seen as a white line through the surrounding heather.

SITING

Mountain or hilltop settings are very common among Irish passage tombs, yet in some instances the prominence chosen is not at a great height but affords extensive views of the surrounding countryside. The three great mounds of Newgrange, Knowth and Dowth, Co. Meath, are situated at an elevation of around 61m, while the main concentrations of sites at Carrowmore, Co. Sligo, and Kilmonaster, Co. Donegal, are relatively low-lying.

The Ballycarty tomb is at an elevation of 29m, yet the reef on which it stands is one of the highest points on the valley floor and affords extensive views westward to the sea and of the flanking mountains to north and south.

Certain aspects of the site can be paralleled elsewhere in Ireland—the presence of later enclosing elements around the reef is repeated at Baltinglass Hill, Co. Wicklow, where the excavated passage tomb stands inside Rathcoran hillfort, at Knocknashee, Co. Sligo, where the Class 1 hillfort encloses two passage tombs, and at Kilmonaster, Co. Donegal, where one of the sites stands inside an enclosing element on Croaghan Hill.

The choice of a site close to a bend in the River Lee can be directly paralleled at Knockroe, Co. Kilkenny, and Knowth, Co. Meath, although a connection between passage tombs and river valleys is not the norm (Eogan 1986, 92).

Even the presence of three other possible cairns, covering similar tombs, on the spur and the resulting arrangement, where the centrally placed cairn is the largest and most impressive while the three to the west are smaller, satellite examples, repeats the layout seen at all the recorded passage tomb cemeteries. However, given the presence of a very large, recently discovered cairn on Knockawaddra Mountain (342m) to the south, any tombs on the reef at Ballycarty may well be satellites themselves (Pl. 28).

AFFINITIES AND PARALLELS WITH THE IRISH PASSAGE TOMB SERIES

Both the Phase 1 cairn and that resulting from the enlargement in Phase 2 are quite small for passage tombs, although sites of similar dimensions are known. Herity (1974, 214–80) recorded eleven sites with diameters of 8m or under, and a further twelve of 9m or under, in his survey of Irish passage tombs. Sites of this size were recorded from most of the areas with high densities of such monuments, and from all of the provinces except Munster (*ibid.*). However, the recently discovered passage tomb at The Lag, Ringarogy Island, Co. Cork, appears to have had a covering mound only 5.5m in diameter (Shee Twohig 1995).

Given that the cairn, in effect, contains three separate monuments, it would seem appropriate to look at the parallels for each phase individually.

Phase 1
The sharp inturning of the kerb at the entrance is recorded at a number of other Irish passage tombs, including Fourknocks 1 and Newgrange K, Co. Meath, and the western tomb at Knockroe, Co. Kilkenny, while the entrance at Duntryleague, Co. Limerick, has also been described as 'funnel-shaped' (Eogan 1986, 102).

However, drystone-walled façades are uncommon in Ireland—the court tomb at Behy, Co. Mayo, being the only example among this class of megalith—and the usual technique involves the use of orthostats or orthostats and dry walling in a post-and-panel arrangement (Fig. 17).

Revetment walls built on the kerbs of passage tombs are known from sites such as Cairn T at Loughcrew, Baltinglass (Walshe 1941, 223), Cairn B at Carrowkeel (Macalister *et al.* 1912, 322) and Newgrange Z (O'Kelly *et al.* 1978, 337), to mention but a few.

The quartz revetment/façade at Newgrange serves a similar purpose to that at Ballycarty, yet it is again distinct from the kerb, whereas at Ballycarty the kerb itself, around the western end of the site, is constructed of walling and indistinguishable from the revetment and façade walling.

It has been suggested that the use of revetment walling was necessary where the covering mound was constructed of loose stones and that it is probable that many Irish passage tombs originally had a drum-like appearance rather than the gently sloping mounds visible today (O'Kelly *et al.* 1978, 338). However, a drystone-walled kerb is recorded from Fourknocks 1, and this would appear to be the closest Irish parallel for the drystone façade and partially

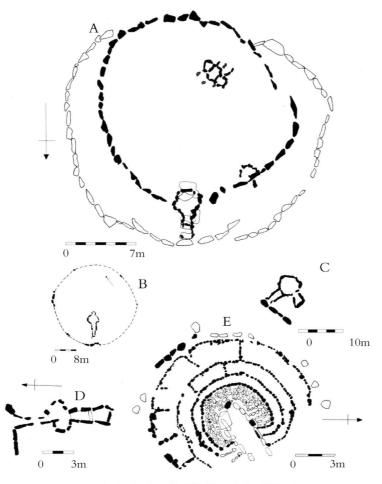

A. Baltinglass, Co. Wicklow (after Walshe)

B. Slieve Gullion, Co. Armagh (after Collins and Wilson)

C. Dowth South, Co. Meath (after O'Kelly)

D. Duntryleague, Co. Limerick (after Herity)

E. Townleyhall, Co. Louth (after Eogan)

Fig. 17—Comparative plans of Baltinglass Hill, Slieve Gullion, Dowth South, Duntryleague and Townleyhall.

walled kerb at Ballycarty (Hartnett 1957, 203).

The drystone-walled passage is also an uncommon feature among Irish passage tombs, where construction using orthostats is the norm. Only at Slieve Gullion, where the passage is short and vestigial, is there evidence for dry walling (Collins and Wilson 1963, 27). Dry walling is, however, used in conjunction with orthostats at a number of sites, including Newgrange and Fourknocks 1.

Cores are recorded from the sites of some passage tombs—Knowth 12, 15, and 16; Newgrange, where the core was a small cairn covered with rounded boulders; Newgrange L and Townleyhall, where the cores were of sand and earth respectively; and Site 27 at Carrowmore, where a circle of stones concentric to the kerb delimited an inner stone packing which may have been a stone core (Burenhult 1980a, 54). However, their use is restricted.

The Phase 1 chamber appears to have been subcircular and 2.86m in diameter. While this form of chamber is not common in Irish passage tombs, it is known, e.g. at the central chamber of Dowth South, Fourknocks 1 and Cairn T at Loughcrew. The closest Irish parallels for the Ballycarty example are Chamber 1 at Baltinglass Hill, Co. Wicklow, where the chamber is between 2.14m and 2.33m in diameter (Walshe 1941), and the small tomb under a 7m-diameter cairn at Site W in the Loughcrew cemetery, where the shortness of the passage is very much in the style of the Ballycarty arrangement.

However, in the event that the area of burnt clay extending outside the conjectural line of the now-destroyed northern side of the chamber is evidence of a destroyed recess at this point, then the chamber at Dowth South would be a very close parallel for Ballycarty.

The laying down of a deliberate floor, as appears to have been done at Ballycarty, is not common amongst Irish passage tombs, although a number of examples, such as Townleyhall, show extensive evidence of pre-tomb activity. Paving is known from a small number of sites, such as Site 14 at Knowth, Fourknocks 1 and Slieve Gullion. However, the closest parallel for the burnt redeposited boulder clay at Ballycarty is to be found at Baltinglass, where Walshe recorded a burnt yellow clay over large areas of the site (Walshe 1941, 227).

The burning of the underlying boulder clay at Baltinglass may have been due to site clearance or may have had some ritual purpose, as may the sequence of events at Ballycarty. However, the actual removal and redeposition of the clay is, so far, unparalleled among Irish passage tombs.

Fourknocks 1 is the only Irish passage tomb for which a wooden roof, in tandem with a corbelled structure, has been proposed, and here the roof was supported by a single massive post placed slightly off-centre in the large, subcircular central chamber (Hartnett 1957, 212). Indeed, the placing of the post at Fourknocks in line with the side wall of the passage rather than centrally in the chamber is similar to the position occupied by the rock-cut depression, for the Phase 2/3 chamber, in relation to the Phase 1 passage.

A single post-hole was also uncovered at the centre of the chamber of Site 27 at Carrowmore, but the excavator felt that it was used for laying out the tomb rather than as a support for any wooden structure (Burenhult 1980a, 21).

Phase 2

The major alterations undertaken during the second phase of activity at the site completely changed the main structural features of the tomb—the passage, the chamber and the entrance area.

The passage of the Phase 2 monument, while partially using existing bedrock outcrop, was constructed of low slabs/boulders set on edge, in the style of the vast majority of Irish passage tombs. The extant lintel clearly shows how large overhanging slabs were placed directly on the side walls, in order to shorten the span of the passage, with the lintels spanning the distance between the overhanging slabs. This method of roofing is also well documented and requires little comment.

The possible Phase 2 chamber (the exact shape, form and structure of the Phase 2 chamber are uncertain), D-shaped and drystone-built, was probably a fully corbelled structure. However, even in its original state it was very small and, though its shape would place it with the small group of Irish sites having circular or polygonal chambers, it is difficult to parallel among Irish passage tombs. Indeed, the closest parallel for the chamber shape is at Bryn Celli Ddu in Anglesey, where the chamber was 2.4m wide in contrast to the 1.1m width of the Ballycarty chamber, and this parallel would be even closer if, as is possible, the Phase 2 chamber was slab-lined rather than drystone-built.

The final addition to the site in Phase 2 was the slab/block-built façade, unparalleled

Pl. 29—The excavated tomb from the north; the curve of the Phase 2 façade can be clearly seen.

amongst the Irish series. While, as has already been shown, curved, funnel-shaped or crescentic entrance features are known, they are always formed by altering the line of the kerb and, as such, are an extension of the kerb.

The secondary façade at Ballycarty articulates with no other feature of the tomb but the secondary passage, although it would seem that the drystone-walled U-shaped setting, which curved back from the southern tip of the façade and helped retain the packing behind that portion of the façade which overran the original cairn, also connected the façade back to the original kerb (Pl. 29).

The alterations during Phase 2, in particular the greater length of passage and the reuse of the bedrock outcrop from Phase 1, necessitated the extension of the cairn to the west. Such an extension can be paralleled at Baltinglass, where, following the building of Chamber 1, which closely parallels the primary chamber at Ballycarty, further construction necessitated an enlargement of the cairn and the construction of an almost completely new kerb (Walshe 1941, 232–3). Tomb enlargement is also recorded at Newgrange K, where the primary passage was increased in length by 3m, but again a new kerb was constructed around the enlarged monument (O'Kelly *et al.* 1978, 281).

The Phase 2 façade at Ballycarty undoubtedly fulfilled the same function as the shorter, more roughly built façade of the Phase 1 monument, but it has more in common with the court feature of Irish court tombs than with any feature encountered in the passage tomb series.

Phase 3

The alterations to the site at this time were all centred on the passage, although it has already been noted that the small, D-shaped, drystone-built chamber may also relate to this phase of activity. The realignment of the more westerly, front half of the Phase 2 passage involved a change from slab/boulder side walls to drystone walling, which, as has already been shown, is known in some form from a small number of Irish passage tombs.

The main effects of this realignment were to change the orientation of the passage entrance from west to west-north-west and to create a slight dogleg in the passage at the point where the slab/boulder-built Phase 2 passage and the drystone-walled Phase 3 passage merge.

The work may have been undertaken in order to facilitate a reorientation of the passage entrance and, while the presence of more than one passage and chamber in a number of tombs clearly illustrates more than one passage orientation at an individual site, the reorientation of an existing passage is not easy to parallel.

The passage at Knowth 16 was realigned, but rather than being undertaken for the sole reason of reorientating the entrance, this work was necessitated by the damage caused to the tomb during the construction of the great mound of Knowth 1 (Eogan 1984, 120), while the passage at Newgrange K was lengthened but retained the same orientation as the original (O'Kelly *et al.* 1978, 280–1).

In general terms, all the structural features of each phase of activity at Ballycarty, with the notable exception of the secondary façade, can be paralleled among known Irish passage tombs. The secondary façade is problematic and, while it may simply have been a one-off solution to the problems caused by the cairn extension rather than a design-motivated construction, it can really only be paralleled by the court feature of Irish court tombs, now the only one of the four main megalithic tomb types unrecorded in County Kerry.

However, the presence of a feature more usual on a court tomb may indicate a knowledge of such tombs and their structure. Indeed, it has been suggested that all four tomb types were being built at more or less the same time, that many borrowings took place, and that within each type there were experiments and elaborations (O'Kelly 1981, 124). The Phase 2 façade, as well as the multi-period nature of the Ballycarty tomb, would seem to confirm this suggestion.

FOREIGN PARALLELS AND AFFINITIES

As noted by Eogan (1992, 122), the simple round chamber with passage is rare in Ireland, yet this simple form is the most widespread, being found right along the Atlantic seaboard (Lynch 1975, fig. 7). The chamber and passage arrangements at Ballycarty fall into this group of simple round- or polygonal-chambered tombs and, given the widespread use of these types of chamber outside Ireland, parallels are numerous, particularly for the Phase 1 monument.

Within the Breton series these simple chambers are regarded as the beginning of the sequence, and examples of the round chamber are common—Kermaric and La Table des Marchands—while the subcircular chamber at Quelvezin is entered through a very short passage, reminiscent of Cairn W at Loughcrew and the Phase 1 monument at Ballycarty.

Indeed, the chamber of simple Breton tombs is often set asymmetrically in relation to the passage, as would also seem to be the case in the Phase 1 monument at Ballycarty.

The D-shaped chamber of the third, and possibly the second, phase at Ballycarty can also be paralleled among the Breton series, though on a much larger scale, at sites such as L'Ile Longue, Dissignac and Colpo.

The use of drystone walling within the chamber and passage, either in tandem with orthostats or as the sole method of construction, is also known in Brittany, while the use of drystone-walled revetments around the cairn is common.

In Iberia the use of dry walling in the passage and chamber is also known, with the tomb at Cueva de Romeral, in the Antequera cemetery, near Malaga, being almost completely built in this technique. Here too the simple round chamber is well documented; the famous cemetery of Los Millares, near Almeira, is composed of around 50 east-facing tombs with short passages entering small circular chambers, each in a small round cairn.

Indeed, the size of chamber and covering cairn in the Los Millares cemetery bears close comparison with the Phase 1 monument at Ballycarty, while the possibility that the Phase 1 chamber at Ballycarty had a wooden roof, similar to that proposed for Fourknocks 1, can be paralleled in the tombs at Praia des Macas and Baranqueta.

Many of the features of the Ballycarty tomb can also be paralleled in Scotland. Crescentic or funnel-shaped façades and façades constructed wholly or partially in drystone walling, as in the Phase 1 monument at Ballycarty, are known, as is the use of dry walling in chambers and passages (Henshall 1972, 38–45).

The simple circular or polygonal chamber can be seen at sites such as Carmahome on Arran, The Ord North in Sutherland, and Marrogh on Uist, where the tomb also has a funnel-shaped entrance. Indeed, a number of the tombs on Uist have this simple chamber.

The Clava cairns, which themselves are isolated within the Scottish series and display the cemetery grouping so characteristic of Irish passage tombs, also display the simple circular chamber plan and bear comparison with the Phase 1 monument at Ballycarty.

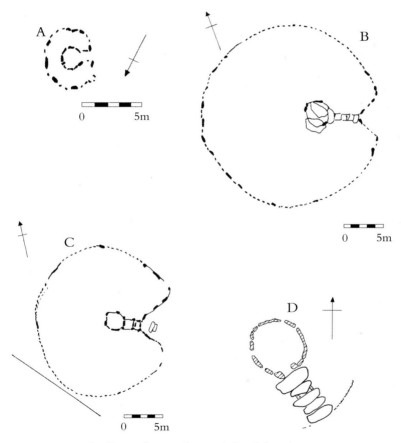

A. Carmahome, Arran (after Mann)
B. Marrogh, Uist (after Henshall)
C. Rudh' an Dunain, Skye (after Scott)
D. Kermaric, Brittany

Fig. 18—Comparative plans of Carmahome, Marrogh, Rudh' an Dunain and Kermaric.

49

However, the most striking parallel is to be found at Rudh' an Dunain on Skye, where a short passage leads into an antechamber and then to a circular chamber. Henshall (1972, 486) has considered the possibility that the antechamber was originally a very short passage which was later extended, and if this is the case the parallel with Ballycarty is even clearer (Fig. 18).

Henshall compared this site to Chamber 1 at Baltinglass, Co. Wicklow, which is a close parallel for the Phase 1 monument at Ballycarty. All three have the simple circular or polygonal chamber and all three cairns have been extended to encompass later alterations. In fact Henshall (*op. cit.*, 257) sees the extension of the cairn at Rudh' an Dunain as indicative of an early date.

Rudh' an Dunain has a south-east-facing, funnel-shaped forecourt with orthostatic façade, and while the forecourt cannot be paralleled at Baltinglass 1 it can be paralleled at Ballycarty, as can the general dimensions of the chamber and the suggested primary passage. Indeed, a number of the tombs in Henshall's Hebridean Group display simple chambers within small round cairns which were later extended, and a number of the tombs also display funnel-shaped or crescentic forecourts (*ibid.*, 245).

It is clear that the basic plan of the Ballycarty tomb can be paralleled across a wide area of Atlantic Europe and that in some cases these parallels can extend beyond the plan of the tomb and into the actual history of the site.

However, it is in the use of a basic chamber plan that the parallels are most clearly defined, and the ease with which such comparisons can be made outside Ireland points up the difficulty in making such comparisons within the country.

The small number of tombs utilising these basic chamber plans does not constitute sufficient evidence for denying the simpler forms the primacy they have been accorded elsewhere in Europe. The fact that the small number of recorded chambers, of simple form, are so widely dispersed within Ireland argues against any regional bias or persistence of outmoded designs, but rather suggests a short-lived use of the simple chamber plan over a wide area.

THE FINDS

The finds from passage tombs have been regarded as an 'unchanging assemblage' (Herity 1974, 86), and yet the elements which are taken to be part of this assemblage—Carrowkeel-type pottery, mushroom-headed pins, beads, stone or chalk balls, pendants and pendant miniatures—have not been found at a number of sites. Indeed, in his 1974 survey of Irish passage tombs, Herity recorded the full assemblage at only a small proportion of sites, while in most cases only elements of the assemblage have been recorded. Pottery, for instance, is only recorded from around 20 tombs, and Eogan (1986, 140) has suggested that its absence from closed contexts, such as Knowth 16 and Fourknocks 1, indicates that there was no practice of placing pottery in every tomb.

The disturbed nature of the Ballycarty tomb has meant that, apart from water-rolled quartz and red sandstone and the stone bead, no finds were recovered from the burial chambers but only from the surrounding cairn.

The stone pendant (96E138:55) is not directly paralleled by finds from other passage tombs, even though beads of stone are recorded quite often. This may well be due to the fact that the pendant's shape and form are the result of natural processes, and only the perforation is the result of man's intervention. However, the fact that the pits and depressions on the pendant's surface are the result of the action of marine sponges implies that the stone was originally retrieved at a coastal location.

The pendant was recovered from a layer of black soil which occurred only within the Phase 3 chamber and part of the passage, and which also contained the bulk of the cremated bone from the site. However, given the disturbed nature of the site, this may not be conclusive evidence that the pendant was part of the burial deposit.

There is much more conclusive evidence relating to those water-rolled pieces of quartz and red sandstone found within the Phase 1 chamber. One of the quartz pebbles, all three of the red sandstone pebbles and the sandstone disc show clear evidence of having been subjected to fire; their presence inside the chamber suggests that they were originally part of the burial deposit in that chamber and may well have been cremated with the remains.

The two hemispheres of quartz conglomerate and red sandstone found in the fill of the Phase 2/3 chamber had also been subjected to intense heat, which probably caused an originally subspherical water-rolled stone to break in half. A fourth water-rolled quartz pebble was found in a disturbed context outside the chamber, and two highly polished limestone pebbles were found inside the kerb on the northern side of the site. All these stones may also originally have been part of a burial deposit.

Interestingly, the cairn itself produced large quantities of halved and quartered water-rolled red sandstone pebbles, which would appear to have been shattered by heat.

That some of these water-rolled red sandstone and quartz stones may have had the same function as the chalk and stone balls found in some passage tombs has already been suggested (Herity 1974, 136), yet the exact function of the balls and naturally rounded pebbles is unknown. It may be that some of the larger stone examples, such as those from Loughcrew F and L, were used to crush the cremated bones and were then deposited with the burial. This process might also explain the presence of stone basins at some sites, and the two depressions on one side of the upper of the two basins from the east recess at Newgrange may have held spheroid stones used to crush cremated bone in the basin.

The antler disc bead (96E138:26), while not a wholly diagnostic find from passage tombs, does represent the only find of antler, a material found commonly on other sites (mushroom-headed pins), from the site. The find can be paralleled: a bone disc bead of similar size was recovered from the chamber at Newgrange (O'Kelly 1982, 195), while a bone disc bead was also recovered from Site 15 at Knowth, where it was associated with a burial deposit and had been burnt.

The large red sandstone block (96E138:43) which may have functioned as an anvil was found at the western limit of the excavation; it probably relates to the same period as the finds of iron slag from around the cairn and in the pit on its northern side, and may be evidence of metalworking on the site. A charcoal sample from the pit, which contained large amounts of iron slag, produced a radiocarbon date of 1331 ± 39, which gives a calibrated date of AD 641–733 (UB-4166).

The fragmentary millstone (96E138:21 A & B) was recovered at a similar stratigraphic level to the two ringed pins, discussed below. The fragments, which show clear evidence of picking and dressing, suggest that the original diameter of the stone was between 0.85m and 1m. Given the radiocarbon date from the area of the site where the fragments were recovered (Sample 4, Appendix 6) and the dates of the ringed pins from a similar level, the stone is likely to have come from a horizontal mill which was probably situated somewhere nearby on the River Lee.

The two bronze ringed pins are of recognisable types which have been the subject of study, most recently by Fanning (1994).

The spiral-ringed baluster-headed pin (96E138:13) is of a type which had largely gone out of fashion by the early Viking period, yet two examples, from counties Down and

Antrim respectively, were found at excavated levels which may be as late as the eleventh century AD (Fanning 1994, 14). In general, the baluster-headed sub-type is regarded as one of the earliest known forms of spiral-ringed pin in Ireland, and it has been suggested that spiral-ringed pins originated in Ireland as early as the fifth century, with a floruit in the seventh and eighth centuries (Fanning 1983, 330; Kelly 1986, 195).

The stirrup-ringed pin (96E138:2) is a very closely dated type, owing to the fact that 68 of the 75 complete examples known are from dated levels within Dublin city. The earliest stratified examples from Dublin can be dated to the first quarter of the eleventh century, and the Dublin evidence also raises the possibility that the type continued in use into the twelfth century (Fanning 1994, 43–4).

Interestingly, of the finds of this type of pin from native Irish contexts, two complete pins and a 'spare' pin have been found in County Kerry, at Skellig Michael, Ardfert Cathedral and Church Island, Valentia. Five complete pins of this type were also recovered from the Early Christian period settlement at Knowth, Co. Meath, where the levels were dated to the tenth and eleventh centuries (*ibid.*). The distribution of this pin type is restricted, and County Kerry now accounts for the largest number of such pins outside Dublin and the surrounding counties. Only one other complete pin is known from Munster, and the Ballycarty pin is the only Munster example from a secular context.

These two pins were recovered within 1.5m of each other, directly under the topsoil, yet the baluster-headed example was in a very poor state of preservation and displayed evidence of having been broken in antiquity, while the crutch-headed pin was in remarkably good condition and displayed very little evidence of use. It is therefore possible that the baluster-headed pin was discarded—the finding of a broken millstone and iron slag on top of and around the cairn would indicate the use of this area as a dump—while the crutch-headed pin may have been lost. However, the possibility that the crutch-headed pin was deliberately placed on the cairn cannot be discounted and may even be paralleled by the finds of much later material, such as the Roman coins and objects of Early Christian date which were deposited at Newgrange (O'Kelly 1982, 73–4), from a number of passage tomb sites.

PASSAGE TOMB DISTRIBUTION (Fig. 19)

The passage tomb at Ballycarty is the first example of its type to be recorded in County Kerry, and is the third of the four main megalithic tomb types from the county (the exception being the court tomb). Interestingly, only one example of a portal tomb is recorded from the county, at Killaclohane, near Castlemaine, on the southern side of the Slieve Mish Mountains and only 11km south-west of Ballycarty (Walsh 1997, 10).

In general, the distribution of passage tombs shows a heavy northern bias, with the four great cemeteries of the Boyne Valley, Loughcrew, Carrowkeel and Carrowmore stretching across the country from County Meath in the east to County Sligo in the west. The majority of the 300 or so recorded passage tombs occur north of a line from Wicklow in the east to Sligo in the west.

Passage tombs are uncommon in Munster. Herity (1974) recorded only two definite examples—at Shrough, Co. Tipperary, and Duntryleague, Co. Limerick. He also noted the possibility that a tomb existed on Clear Island, Co. Cork, and that the mountaintop cairns at Deerpark and Temple Hill, Co. Limerick, and Temple Etney (Slievenaman), Co. Tipperary, cover similar tombs (*ibid.*, 261–2). There is also the small group of so-called 'entrance graves' near Tramore, Co. Waterford, which Eogan (1986, 90) describes as simple passage tombs unlikely to belong to the main sequence. The most recently discovered tomb in Munster

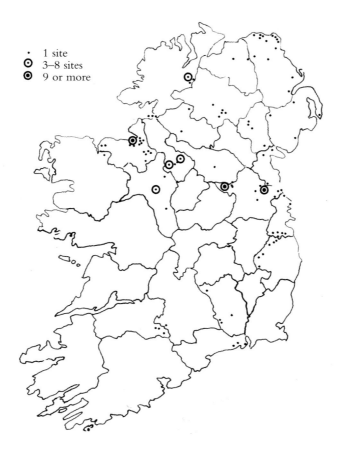

- · 1 site
- ⊙ 3–8 sites
- ◉ 9 or more

Fig. 19—Distribution of Irish passage tombs.

is that recorded at The Lag, Ringarogy Island, Co. Cork (Shee Twohig 1995).

If one accepts that the Tramore group are distinct from true passage tombs and takes into account only those examples proven to be passage tombs, the total figure for Munster, prior to the Ballycarty excavations, is four—Shrough, Duntryleague, Ringarogy Island and the probable tomb that existed on Clear Island.

Any addition to such a small total would be significant, and it is even more so when one considers that it occurs well outside the areas of the other sites and pushes the distribution into north-west Munster. More importantly, the presence of at least two similar sites on the reef at Ballycarty and a further 20–30 cairns on similar reefs in the valley floor and on the slopes of the flanking mountains raises the distinct possibility that the Lee Valley is home to a sizeable cemetery grouping.

Indeed, there is little doubt that two of the cairns on the reef at Ballycarty do contain similar tombs—one has been so denuded that the structural stones of the passage and chamber can be seen, while the shape of the collapsed area in the centre of the central cairn clearly indicates a chamber and passage arrangement—while the large cairn on Knockawaddra Mountain must, given its size, be seen as covering a passage tomb.

The presence of a single tomb, now the most westerly recorded example in Europe, significantly alters the distribution of passage tombs, but the presence of a cemetery group, of any size, has implications not only for the distribution of such monuments but possibly also for the point of origin of the tradition and for the chronological sequence within the

Irish series. However, in the absence of concrete dating evidence from the tomb these possibilities can only be advanced through further excavation in the area.

The presence of a passage tomb near Tralee also has implications for the large number of unopened mountaintop cairns recorded in Cork and Kerry. In a Kerry context it opens up a new avenue of approach to the question of the poor prehistoric burial record in the county, which until recently consisted of around 25 recorded wedge tombs, the single portal tomb, ten or so boulder burials, a number of unclassified megalithic tombs, and three possible cist burials.

This corpus of burial monuments has recently been expanded by the discovery of some late Bronze Age pit burials to the north of Tralee (Dunne 1998) but is still relatively small, given the presence of man on the Dingle Peninsula during the late Mesolithic (Woodman *et al.* 1984), the evidence for early copper exploitation in the county and the large number of Bronze Age ritual monuments which have been recorded on the peninsulas (Cuppage 1986, 37–54; O'Sullivan and Sheehan 1996, 45–72).

The unopened mountaintop cairns may contain the burial evidence that appears to be lacking from the archaeological record of County Kerry, and, more intriguingly, the possibility exists that this evidence may comprise passage tombs or hybridised megalithic tombs in the general passage tomb tradition.

DATING OF THE PASSAGE TOMB

Six samples were sent for radiocarbon dating, but unfortunately all date episodes of later disturbance rather than the periods of the tomb's construction and original use. This is not surprising, given that none of the samples came from a secure context and those contexts that were sealed failed to produce any material suitable for radiocarbon dating.

Some of the charcoal recovered from the fill of the Phase 3 passage and chamber may relate to this period of use, but there is little doubt that much of the material relates to later activity and therefore the dates from this material must be seen as unsafe.

Even the flint and chert artefacts recovered from the site were, in many cases, exposed near the surface owing to disturbance, and the assemblage as a whole is not sufficiently diagnostic for any definite determination of date. However, Professor Peter Woodman, in his report on the lithic assemblage (see Appendix 1), felt that, on the basis of size, the use of invasive retouch and the presence of a possible slug knife, the assemblage would fit comfortably into a Bronze Age context (although it should be noted that a slug knife was recovered from a primary context in the mound of Knowth 13). He also pointed out that some of the material could very well be of Neolithic date, and that no determination could be made with any degree of certainty.

The stone bead/pendant and antler disc bead are similarly undiagnostic, and thus there is no hard dating evidence for any of the three main phases of activity at the site.

However, the identification of the megalithic tomb as a passage tomb and the numerous parallels with other Irish passage tombs suggest a date in the late Neolithic, while the fact that the extant chambers are of the simple round or polygonal type would, in the proposed development sequences for Breton (L' Helgouac'h 1965) and Scottish (Henshall 1972, 257) tombs, be seen as indicative of an early stage in passage tomb development.

The developmental sequence in Ireland is not as clearly defined and round chambers are not common in the Irish series. Nevertheless, while acknowledging the unreliability of typology for dating purposes, Eogan (1986, 212) has suggested a comparison between the round-chambered tomb of Baltinglass 1 and the early round or polygonal chambers of the western European series. Baltinglass 1 is one of the closest parallels for the Phase 1 tomb at Ballycarty, and a similar comparison with early European sites could also be made.

The presence of a curved façade, most easily paralleled amongst court tombs, might also be indicative of date. There is, in some areas, a distributional overlap between passage and court tombs, and there may also be a temporal overlap. The two tomb types appear to be mutually exclusive, with little evidence of borrowings by one from the other.

However, the long cairn of Site E at Carrowkeel may be evidence of a court tomb feature borrowed by a passage tomb-builder, while in areas more removed from the main distributions of both types, such as Kerry, greater hybridisation, owing to experimentation and a dilution of the original design concepts, might be likely to occur.

As already noted, the radiocarbon determinations seem to be indicative of later disturbance, and in a number of cases they tie in closely with the few datable artefacts from the excavations. The date of cal. AD 641–773 from the charcoal- and slag-filled pit on the north side of the cairn and the date of cal. AD 547–655 from a charcoal-rich layer overlying the Phase 2/3 passage and chamber closely match the dating proposed by Fanning (1983, 330) for the development and use of spiral-ringed, baluster-headed pins. The fact that this pin was recovered directly under the topsoil places it at a stratigraphically late phase in the life of the cairn. Similarly, the radiocarbon date from the Phase 3 chamber (cal. AD 1020–1210) matches the proposed dating for the stirrup-ringed, crutch-headed pin and the date range for the use of horizontal mills, the probable origin of the broken millstone. Again, both artefacts were recovered directly under the topsoil covering the cairn.

The date from the abundant wood charcoal in the realigned section of the Phase 3 passage was cal. 96 BC–AD 75, and is the only date for which an artefact parallel is unavailable; however, the possibility exists that this episode of disturbance relates to the enclosure of the reef.

Thus we can say that substantial activity and consequent disturbance took place in the vicinity of the tomb during the periods centred on AD 1100, AD 700 and during the middle of the Iron Age.

The lack of dating evidence for the tomb and the fact that no similar sites in the immediate area have been excavated cause problems in placing the tomb in a chronological context and raise many questions. Yet while passage tombs elsewhere in Ireland are generally dated to the later Neolithic, there is the intriguing possibility that this tomb type and its associated burial rite persisted into the Bronze Age in this area of the south-west.

However, the recent stray find of a hollow-based flint arrowhead in the general area of the large cairn on Knockawaddra Mountain and the discovery of a rectangular Neolithic house, with associated finds of flint and Western Neolithic pottery, on a limestone reef in Cloghers townland (L. Dunne, pers. comm.), 4km north-west of Ballycarty, clearly show that there was Neolithic activity in the valley.

There are a number of similar sites to the Ballycarty cairn/tomb, both on the reef at Ballycarty and in the surrounding valley, and it is clear that only further excavation in the area will help to place the Ballycarty tomb in the Irish passage tomb series and confirm the existence of a probable cemetery grouping in this area of County Kerry.

7.   THE RAMPART

As noted already, two very different construction techniques were used in the section of the rampart exposed at the western end of the reef. At either end of the 49m-long section cutting off the western end of the reef, portions of rampart were uncovered, faced internally and externally, the intervening space being filled with stones and soil. Most of the rampart is of a much more random construction, with alternating layers of earth and stone piled up on the crest of a rise in the bedrock.

The surface appearance of the lengthy stretches of rampart visible on the northern and southern sides of the reef is similar to that of the western rampart prior to excavation, but since these ramparts are steeper, scarped sharply into the natural slope of the reef and quite wide, they are more likely to be of the more random construction.

The more northerly of the faced sections is cut into the underlying boulder clay, while the more southerly faced section and all of the randomly constructed rampart show no evidence of foundations or wall cuts and rest directly on the underlying bedrock (Pl. 30).

Pl. 30—The rampart, looking north toward the cairn; the line of stones denoting the facing of the central wall can clearly be seen.

This is not the only difference between the two walled sections. The more southerly seamlessly links into the more randomly constructed rampart section, whereas the northern section seems more like a later addition, with no effort made to incorporate it into the earlier structure. The northern section was better built than the southern, while the material around the southern wall had the appearance of being placed there deliberately rather than being the result of collapse.

This indicates that the rampart had at least two construction phases, while the fact that it curves sharply to the west, to avoid the tomb, before continuing a northerly course clearly demonstrates that it post-dates the construction of the passage tomb and covering cairn. Given that the more northerly section also runs over the innermost of the ramparts, which runs along the northern side of the reef, it clearly post-dates this construction also.

CONSTRUCTION HISTORY AND FUNCTION

The ramparts around the reef are in general very denuded, yet the lack of wall trenches or foundations in the excavated sections suggests that they could never have achieved any great height, although their placement on natural crests in the bedrock helps to give the exterior an exaggerated height in many places.

This, coupled with the lack of ditches, would have made the ramparts of very little defensive value. However, early map editions record that the surrounding land was very marshy up until the recent past, and the only dry approach to the reef would have been from the east. This may have made it unnecessary to built massive defensive ramparts, yet one would expect to find some substantial defensive element cutting off the eastern approach and this is the very area where even the low ramparts visible elsewhere are difficult to discern.

The presence of at least two and possibly three ramparts on the northern side of the reef would also point to a defensive function, while the vague traces of a possible ditch between two of these northern ramparts may indicate that rock-cut ditches, now filled with material from the collapsed ramparts, exist on the unexcavated sides of the reef.

It may be that the purpose of the extant ramparts was to define an area rather than to defend it, and that the focus of attention was on what was inside these enclosing elements rather than on the ramparts themselves.

Given the similar lack of wall trenches or foundations and the way in which the southern walled section links into the more randomly constructed rampart, it is probable that these two sections are coeval even though two different construction styles are used. It would also seem that the walled section was deliberately built as the core of a wider rampart constructed immediately afterwards.

There is no apparent reason for the presence of a core at this point, but the fact that it occurs where the rampart has just curved round from the northern side of the reef and where the slope in the bedrock is particularly sharp may offer a possible answer. Faced cores may be found at other points in the ramparts where stability was a constructional problem.

The presence of an area clear of stone and protruding bedrock and containing only boulder clay, immediately inside the rampart, from the cairn to its southern extent, may, as already suggested, be either evidence of a deliberate walkway or the result of clearance to facilitate the construction of the rampart. The fact that this feature runs along the inside of both the piled rampart and that with the walled core would also indicate that they are contemporary; equally, the fact that it does not appear inside the rampart running from the northern side of the cairn would seem to suggest that this is a later addition.

The failure to uncover any earlier rampart structure in this area would seem to imply that, unless any earlier rampart was effectively removed prior to the construction of the later double-faced core wall, there was a deliberate gap, of indeterminate length, in the rampart between the north side of the cairn's secondary façade and the rampart running along the north side of the reef.

However, given that the area in question is one of the most disturbed on the whole site, with evidence of activity from the construction of the cairn, through the various episodes of cairn disturbance and up to the very recent past (modern iron fence pegs driven into and around the double-faced core wall), there is very little evidence on which to base any assessment of what, if any, features pre-dated the extant wall.

DATING

The finds from the rampart sections—clay pipes, animal bones (mainly rabbit), iron slag, and some flint, chert and possible crucible fragments from beneath the rampart—are not of great help in trying to date either type of construction. However, the fact that the second-highest concentration of slag on the site and all the slag finds from the rampart, as well as the two possible crucible fragments, came from underneath the wall collapse in the most northerly section is of note. A radiocarbon date of cal. AD 641–773 from charcoal in a pit containing similar slag may indicate a *terminus post quem* for this section of the rampart.

However, apart from this possible link between the pit containing slag and the slag from the northern rampart section, the fact that the rampart post-dates the cairn and that some sections are earlier than others, there is no specific dating evidence for the rampart.

Structurally, the use of faced, rubble core construction can be paralleled at many sites, such as the stone forts at Cahercommaun, Co. Clare, and Dun Aonghusa on Inis Mór. The fort at Cahercommaun is dated to around AD 800–900 on the basis of a brooch find, although material datable to the Roman period, the pre-Roman Iron Age and even earlier was noted (Hencken 1938, 2), while one of the double-faced core walls, which was later incorporated into a more substantial wall, at Dun Aonghusa has a *terminus post quem* of cal. 900–540 BC (Cotter 1995, 7).

The incorporation of lines of boulders and slabs, forming a central core, into the massive ramparts at Mooghaun, Co. Clare, and the use of low stone and earth banks as primary rampart structures at the same site may offer a parallel for the walled core at the southern end of the Ballycarty rampart. The use of the centrally placed boulders and slabs at Mooghaun was radiocarbon-dated to cal. 1260–930 BC (Grogan 1996a).

Indeed, the excavation of a second hillfort in this area of County Clare, at Clenagh, revealed ramparts of similar size and construction to the more random construction revealed in the centrally placed sections at Ballycarty (Grogan 1996b). Interestingly, this site is similar in size to the enclosed area at Ballycarty and possibly encloses a small cairn.

These parallels clearly illustrate the long currency of certain rampart-building techniques, most notably the use of double-faced core walls. However, the incorporation of such walls or other stabilising features into larger, more randomly constructed ramparts and the construction of large piled ramparts without such stabilising features seem to be in vogue during the late prehistoric period. The meandering nature of the long stretches of rampart along the sides of the reef may also indicate a prehistoric date.

8.   BURIAL AND RITUAL PRACTICE AT BALLYCARTY

THE BURIAL RITE

The only two bone fragments which were identified as human had been cremated, and therefore it is reasonably safe to assume that this was the burial rite at the site. However, even if all the unidentified cremated bone recovered from the site proved to be human, there is much less than would result from the cremation of a single individual. While this can easily be explained through disturbance of the site in antiquity and probably up to quite recently, there may be other possible explanations.

The presence of a clearly defined court area in all three phases of activity at the site may be seen as providing a ritual space. The smaller, more constricted court of Phase 1 is probably indicative of the numbers of people meant to view or participate in the burial rituals, while the larger, more open court of Phase 2/3 would seem to indicate a wider audience and increased participation.

The main features of the court area are the five rock-cut pits, one of which relates to much later activity at the site. However, the four pits closest to the tomb entrance were probably used in whatever rituals took place within the defined space of the court.

The presence of cremated bone fragments (unidentifiable except for two dog teeth and a bone from a barn owl) in at least two of the pits, as well as the presence of ash and flecks of charcoal in all four, would suggest that these pits were used either as crematoria or as repositories for token burial. Two of the pits show evidence of having been subjected to heat, while the evidence relating to the remaining two is less clear. The pits are quite small and there is little doubt that, if used as cremation sites, they could only have accommodated minimal remains for burning.

Given this fact and the lack of definite evidence for the cremation of remains within the tomb, it would seem either that the actual cremation of the remains took place elsewhere or that only small quantities of bone were cremated and placed in the tomb.

This leaves the question of what happened to the rest of the skeletal remains. It is possible that the rest of the cremated body was buried elsewhere, but it is equally possible that only part of the skeletal material was cremated, the remaining bones being maintained as relics of the ancestor or buried in other sites of the period, as has been suggested by Barrett (1988) and Bradley (1998).

THE GRAVE-GOODS

The number of finds from the actual chambers was quite small. Finds from the Phase 1 chamber consisted of three water-rolled quartz pebbles, one of which appears to have been subjected to fire, three water-rolled red sandstone pebbles, all of which appear to have been burnt, and a single red sandstone disc, again with evidence of burning. The four fossils recovered from the Phase 1 chamber could also be seen as grave-goods. They are discussed below in more detail.

The finds from the Phase 2/3 passage and chamber consisted of a single stone bead or pendant and two pieces of red sandstone, which seem to be the remains of water-rolled pebbles that had shattered during subjection to intense heat.

The antler disc bead, found just outside the Phase 2/3 chamber, on the north side of the site, was probably also part of the grave deposits.

As already noted, the stone bead/pendant bears evidence of action by marine sponges and must have originated at a coastal location, while the burning of some of the quartz and red sandstone water-rolled pebbles would indicate that they were cremated with the human remains and subsequently placed in the tomb.

However, the assemblage from the burial chambers is small, and while material may well have been removed or destroyed during the various phases of activity at the site, it is also possible that this is the sum total of the grave-goods.

ANIMALS AND RITUAL

As with most sites of this type, a sizeable number of animal bones were recovered, a large proportion of which were unidentifiable. However, the bulk of the animal bones belonged to the three main domestic species—cattle, sheep and pig. The site also produced bones of horse and dog, as well as a good assemblage of bird bone.

The large quantities of animal bone and seashells often found in excavations of passage tombs are usually explained as the remains of ritual feasting (Herity 1974, 119), and this is possibly the case as regards most of the faunal assemblage from Ballycarty. However, this does not adequately explain all the animal bones recovered, particularly those from other than the main domestic species. For some of these remains a more specific ritual function seems likely, while the fact that a certain proportion of the animal remains, including bones of the main livestock animals, were cremated may also be evidence of a more specific ritual.

The evidence for horse at the site was based solely on the finding of teeth, including one which was inside the conjectural line of the Phase 1 chamber. While this tooth may be intrusive and the other teeth were found in contexts where they could, again, have been deposited much later, it is possible that they were deliberately deposited during one of the phases of activity at the site. There is also the question as to why only teeth were recovered, and this in itself may point to a ritual deposition.

The evidence is much clearer in relation to the cremated humerus of a sheep-sized animal, recovered from a small pit in the Phase 2/3 passage, and the pair of bird claws (from a large bird, exact species unknown) found in the base of the deepest post-hole inside the Phase 1 chamber. Both of these deposits would seem to be ritual in nature, while the claws from the post-hole are best explained as a foundation deposit.

A similar ritual significance would have to be proposed for the almost complete skeleton of a large dog found at the base of the cairn material, at a point just inside the passage of the Phase 1 chamber and directly behind the southern side wall of the Phase 2/3 passage. This deposit could only have been made during the building of the Phase 2 passage and must have had a considerable ritual significance. Indeed, dog bones were found in contexts relating to all three phases of activity at the site, being also found in the Phase 2/3 passage and in one of the court pits.

The femur of a song-thrush was recovered from a lens of burnt material near the base of the cairn core and, given the weight of material above it, must be viewed as a deliberate deposition during the primary phase of activity at the site.

The remains of at least three individual corncrakes were recovered from the Phase 2/3 passage. While it is possible that they were dragged in by animals, a large proportion of the remains were recovered from a layer of very burnt black soil containing a number of tiny fragments of cremated bone which are likely to be human. Wing bones formed the bulk of the corncrake skeletal remains, and while the disturbed nature of the site leaves the evidence open to question it is possible that these bones were deposited with the burials.

There are parallels both in Ireland and farther afield for the deposition of bird bones with burials in passage tombs. The remains of a plover-sized bird are recorded from one of the chambers of the cruciform passage tomb on Belmore Mountain, Co. Fermanagh, while dog and bird bones are recorded from Tumulus L at Newgrange (Herity 1974, 171).

In Scotland animal bones are recorded from a number of sites, but of special interest are the dog and bird bone (wing bones predominating) recovered from the chambered cairn at Torlin on Arran, the animal bone, including bird, from near one of the chamber orthostats at Rudh' an Dunain on Skye, and the skeletal remains of an adult and immature dog from the chamber at Tulach an T'sionnaich (Henshall 1972, 390, 488, 552).

Probably the most enigmatic find of animal bone from Ballycarty comes from one of the pits in the court area, where a single bone from a barn owl and two dog molars were found with some small fragments of cremated bone which, while unidentifiable, may be human. The material was found in a matrix of grey ash and burnt soil, and only deliberate ritual deposition seems to offer a suitable explanation.

It is interesting that it is almost exclusively bones of dog and birds that were recovered from possible ritual contexts, inviting speculation on the possible importance of these animals to the society which built and later altered the tomb.

The possibility that the dog and certain species of birds, such as barn owl, were tribal totems would explain their inclusion in the rituals associated with the insertion of burials in the tomb and the construction of the monument itself. This raises the question of the deposition and/or cremation of remains from these totem animals with possible human bone in one of the rock-cut pits in the court area, and it is tempting to suggest that this ritual involved consigning the spirit of the deceased to the protection of the tribal totems or investing the life essence of the deceased in the living bodies of the tribe's totemic guardians, thus connecting the veneration of the totems and of the ancestors; however, this is pure speculation.

THE FOSSILS

The most unusual use of animal or plant remains from the Ballycarty site was the deposition of loose, cleaned fossils in and around the Phase 1 chamber. Fossils were recovered from underneath the cairn core and inside the kerb on the southern side of the site. Those four found within the primary chamber were placed directly on the redeposited boulder clay floor, close to the bases of structural stones.

All the fossils recovered were on the southern side of the site but any that may have been placed in similar positions on the northern side would have been disturbed during the various alterations and disturbances of that side of the site.

All the fossil types recovered occur naturally in the limestone rock of the reef, yet there would have been a considerable amount of work involved in extracting and cleaning them without breaking the fossil, and therefore their deposition must have had some ritual significance.

Many theoretical suggestions could be put forward for the deposition of the fossils, but perhaps the most intriguing concerns the shape and form of many of those recovered and their similarity to the concentric circles and spirals so common in the repertoire of the artists who carved designs on the structural stones of tombs in the Boyne Valley and elsewhere. Indeed, the find-spots of the fossils—close to the bases of four stones of the primary chamber and just behind stones of the kerb—are just where one would expect to find decorated stones.

SOLAR EVENTS AND THE PASSAGE ALIGNMENTS

Owing to the relatively low-lying position of the tomb and the presence of a large tract of woodland to the west and north-west, it is difficult to ascertain whether any of the three different passage orientations has a specific solar alignment. However, it can be said that, given the slight dogleg inside the entrance, no sunlight could ever have penetrated to the chamber during Phase 3 of the monument's history.

The western orientation of the passage in Phases 1 and 2 would indicate a general alignment on the setting sun, and observation has shown that during the vernal equinox the sun does set at an angle that would allow sunlight to enter the Phase 1 passage. However, the presence of trees on the summit of a low hill to the west makes this phenomenon impossible to document (Pl. 31).

It can be said that the setting sun, during the vernal equinox, disappears from view behind the low hill 1km to the west. It can also be said that the slope of this hill, facing the passage tomb entrances, is the site of one of six embanked enclosures recently identified around Tralee.

Embanked enclosures are regarded as ritual sites related to henges, and are normally found in lowland river valleys. They are often set within a wider ritual landscape, and an association between such enclosures and passage tombs has been suggested (Stout 1991, 251; Condit and Simpson 1998, 47).

The fact that the tomb can be seen from the embanked enclosure and vice versa is clearly important, as is the siting of the enclosure on the side of a hill behind which the setting sun disappears at certain times of the year. Indeed, a relationship between the two sites seems likely, given the fact that while some alignment with the setting sun is possible for the Phase 1 monument, the Phase 2 passage and the alterations to the entrance during Phase 3 refine the alignment of the tomb with the enclosure, while making any specific solar alignment almost impossible.

Pl. 31—The tomb from the west, showing the Phase 1 passage (behind the façade), the Phase 2 passage (bedrock to right of the Phase 3 passage), and the Phase 3 passage.

This may indicate that the embanked enclosure and the final phase of construction at the passage tomb are contemporary, which, given the dates from the only excavated example of an embanked enclosure, at Monknewtown, Co. Meath (Sweetman 1976, 70–1), would suggest a date of around 2000 BC for this activity.

A RITUAL LANDSCAPE

The limestone reef on which the passage tomb is situated has, as described above, a wealth of other sites on its summit, and is enclosed by up to three stone and earth banks (Fig. 20).

The nature of these other features—cairns, possible henge, possible causeway and enclosures—indicates that the reef was a centre of burial and ritual, while the presence of the embanked enclosure in the townland of Ballyseedy, 1km to the west, links the reef to the surrounding landscape.

Prior to the discovery of the complex at Ballycarty, the area around Tralee was a veritable prehistoric 'blackspot', with only a very small number of *fulachta fiadh* recorded. The artefact record was also quite poor, yet the most important find from the area was of a prehistoric date—the hoard of six bronze horns found in a bog in the townland of Clogherclemin (2.5km east of Tralee) in 1875.

However, since the excavation of the passage tomb at Ballycarty, fieldwork in the valley of the River Lee has identified 106 new sites, nineteen of which are archaeological complexes containing a further 84 separate elements. Most of the sites are found on the south bank of the river at a distance of no more than 2km from its course, while the greatest

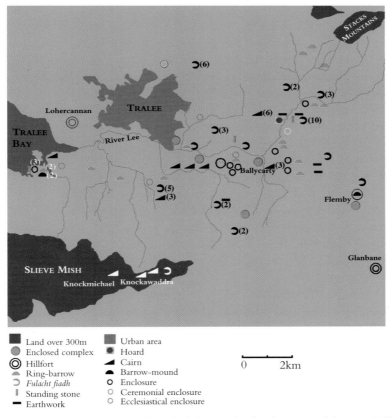

Fig. 20—Distribution of sites identified during the brief survey of the Lee Valley.

Pl. 32—Limestone reef at Manor East; cremated bone, water-rolled quartz and red sandstone were recovered from the site of a cairn destroyed by the building works in the background.

concentrations were in the adjoining townlands of Ballymacthomas, Ballycarty, Ballyseedy and Camp, at the point where the River Lee bends to take its westward course to the sea.

The range of site types was quite small but full of intriguing possibilities. Cairns, *fulachta fiadh* and barrows predominated, but at least five and possibly seven henges, six embanked enclosure-type sites (approximately one fifth of the total identified examples of this site type) and a bivallate hillfort were also identified. In a number of instances different site types were found together, while groupings consisting of a barrow and *fulachta fiadh* were quite common, and in two instances an embanked enclosure was abutted by a ring-barrow.

The discovery of two cairns, one of which is at least 30m in diameter and remains to a height of 9m, just below the summit of Knockawaddra Mountain, 4km south-south-west of Ballycarty, together with the evidence from the reef at Ballycarty itself, the recent recovery of cremated animal and human bone, water-rolled quartz, large quantities of angular quartz and heat-shattered water-rolled red sandstone from the site of a recently destroyed cairn on another enclosed reef, and the evidence from other similar reefs in the area, would suggest that the passage tomb at Ballycarty may be one element in a sizeable passage tomb cemetery.

This suggestion may be substantiated by the identification of six embanked enclosures in the area, given their suggested association with passage tombs and particularly with the tombs of the Boyne Valley (Stout 1991, 251).

It was also noticeable that much of this newly identified material occurred on or around limestone reefs, similar to Ballycarty, and that many of the larger reefs followed the Ballycarty model—cairns, quarry ditches, enclosures and ramparts. In fact 80% of all the limestone outcrops visited in the course of fieldwork were crowned by archaeological features.

While it is impossible to answer the question raised regarding the significance of these geological features and their attraction for the previous inhabitants of the valley, it is possible to see a definite pattern of use of such limestone reefs. Indeed, it is probably the fact that such reefs are not agriculturally viable that has ensured the preservation of most of these remains, and this may be the very reason why they were originally chosen as the sites for so many burial and ritual monuments (Pl. 32).

The results of this brief survey around Tralee suggest that a similar pattern may be repeated in other areas of limestone reef and outcrop. The work of the Discovery Programme in south Clare would seem to provide a very close parallel for the Lee Valley material, and this raises the possibility that there is a very specific 'limestone reef archaeology' which, because of the low level of the remains, has been largely ignored.

Yet in the case of the Lee Valley these limestone reefs appear to have been the main repositories for the prehistory of the area, a prehistory that until recently was conspicuously absent.

However, with the benefit of this information it is possible to see the presence of so many probable burial monuments and ritual-type sites, the deposition of a hoard of six bronze horns, and the recently identified ritual deposition of a broken Early Bronze Age axe type (Connolly 1998) as being indicative of a fairly continuous use of the valley as a place of burial, ritual and probably habitation during the early prehistoric period.

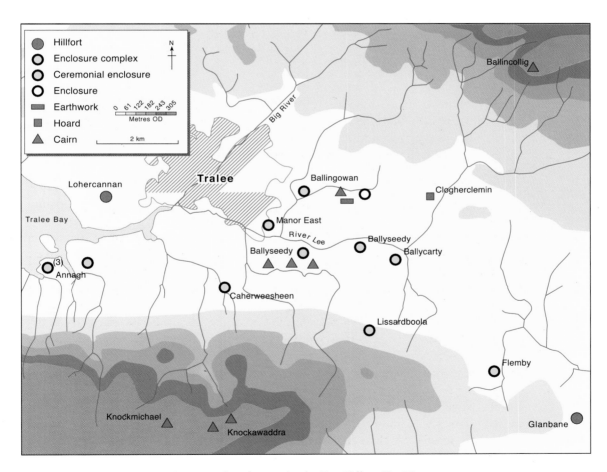

Fig. 21—Ritual enclosures in the Lee Valley, Co. Kerry.

9. CONCLUSION

On the basis of the evidence, there is little doubt that the cairn at Ballycarty covered a small passage tomb, of simple plan, with three main phases of activity. It is also clear that the limestone reef was the site of substantial activity during the prehistoric and historic periods and that its enclosure was a major undertaking.

The site has been severely disturbed during the course of its history and most of the material recovered during the excavation was found in contexts which are undoubtedly not original, while the results of radiocarbon dating identify the periods of later disturbance rather than the construction of the monument. There is therefore no hard dating evidence for any of the three main phases of activity.

However, most of the main structural features of each of the three phases of activity can be paralleled amongst the Irish and European passage tomb series. Indeed, the simple circular chamber of Phase 1 would, in a European context, be taken as an indicator of an early date, yet this type of chamber is uncommon in Ireland.

The tomb at Ballycarty is the most westerly example now recorded and significantly alters the distribution of such sites. Following recent survey and research, it is clear that the valley of the River Lee is home to the most important prehistoric landscape in County Kerry, and that a sizeable component of the archaeology of the valley is composed of small cairns similar to those on the reef at Ballycarty.

The very real possibility that the tomb at Ballycarty is part of a larger cemetery group has major implications for passage tomb distribution, dating and the developmental sequence in Ireland, as well as the origin of the Irish series. Indeed, the possibility that a feature like the Phase 2 façade was a direct borrowing from court tombs raises intriguing questions regarding Irish megalithic tombs as a whole and seriously challenges the suggested exclusivity of the four main megalithic tomb traditions (Pl. 33).

However, without further excavation and research into the sites in the Lee Valley these possibilities must remain in the realm of speculation.

Pl. 33—The tomb from the west-north-west.

APPENDIX 1. THE LITHIC ASSEMBLAGE

PROFESSOR PETER WOODMAN
Department of Archaeology,
University College Cork

FLINT (Fig. 22)

96E138:10 A   This small portion of a flint flake, and B below, were found near the surface of the extant remains of the cairn core, in the redeposited boulder clay (C51) which surrounded the heavy stone packing. The flake is patinated light brown and a mottled blue/white. The piece is so fragmentary that it is impossible to estimate whether it is a portion of a blade or a flake. Maximum length 2cm.

96E138:10 B   This is probably the proximal section of a small blade; it is quite weathered and patinated brown. It is a secondary cortical flake whose left lateral edge is formed by water-rolled cortex. Maximum length 2.1cm.

96E138:14 A   Both A and B, below, were found directly under the topsoil that partially covered the mound of cairn material, on the north side of the court area, which had been removed from the tomb during some period of disturbance. This piece is part of a small flint flake; it is very weathered and patinated deep white with patches of brown staining. Maximum length 1.7cm.

96E138:14 B   This small core could be considered as a bipolar core. It is patinated beige/white but is, by the standards of this assemblage, comparatively unweathered. It has been made from a small water-rolled pebble which has had small, squat flakes removed from either end. Most of the flakes have been removed from one, rather than both, surfaces. Maximum length 2.5cm.

96E138:15   This piece was found in the same area of the site as no. 14 above, and was also directly under the topsoil. It is a small, unpatinated scraper, which may have been made on a small split pebble of flint rather than a flake. The cortical surface is so highly polished that it is reminiscent of *remaniée* flint. The retouch, which is comparatively steep and slightly irregular, extends around virtually 50% of its circumference. Maximum length 2.2cm.

96E138:17   This piece was, again, found in the mound of disturbed cairn material which was piled up on the north side of the court feature. It was within the redeposited boulder clay at the base of the feature. It is a fractured portion of a retouched tool, and is weathered and patinated yellow and blue/white. It would appear to be the lateral edge of a retouched tool. The semi-invasive retouch along the lateral edge of a comparatively thick flake could indicate that it was a portion of a slug knife. Maximum length 2.74cm.

96E138:20   This scraper was found in the redeposited boulder clay which surrounded the extant remains of the cairn core. It has been made from a primary cortical flake which was struck from a water-smoothed nodule. It is weathered and has a mottled white patina. The retouch is mostly semi-invasive and extends across the distal end and along the lateral edge. Maximum length 3.2cm.

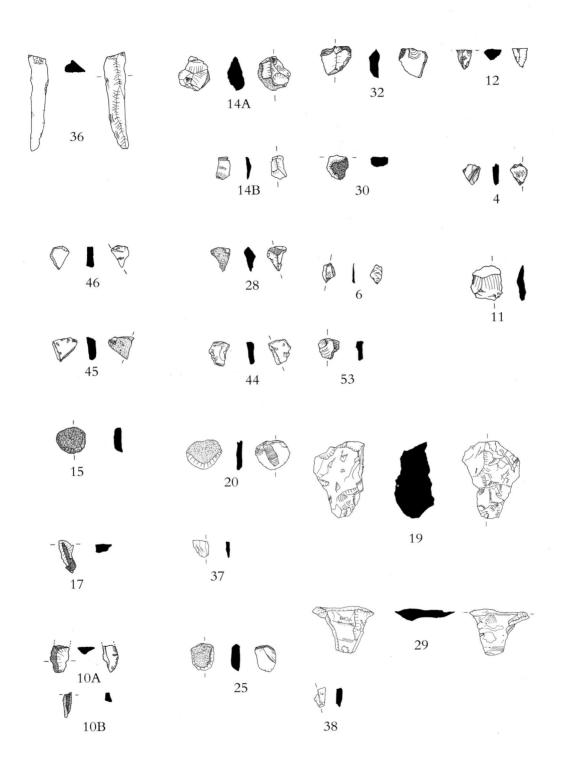

Fig. 22—The lithic material.

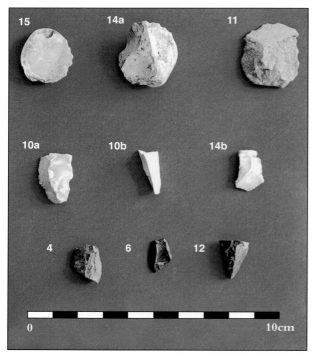

Pl. 34—Stone objects.

96E138:25 This scraper was found in a stony deposit under the lowest course of masonry in the most northerly rampart section. It was made on a large decortical flake or on a split pebble where retouch has significantly reduced its size. It is less weathered than most other pieces in this assemblage and is patinated beige. It is not an 'end' scraper but has comparatively steep retouch around three edges. A flake has been removed from the bulbar surface on the right lateral edge. Maximum length 2.4cm (Pls 34 and 35).

96E138:28 This small portion of a flint flake was found in a burnt layer inside the Phase 2/3 chamber. It is weathered and patinated white and brown. Maximum length 1.93cm.

96E138:30 This small end scraper was found in a very disturbed context on the north side of the cairn. It is quite weathered and has a mottled blue/white patina. It has been made either on a split pebble or a portion of a large primary cortical flake. This small flake has been steeply retouched round much of its circumference, but one edge has a slightly different patina. Maximum length 1.7cm.

96E138:45 This piece was found in the redeposited boulder clay at the very disturbed north side of the cairn. It is a small section of a primary decortical flake made from a water-rolled nodule. The bulbar surface is patinated grey, but as the flake has fractured since deposition the two fractured surfaces are unpatinated. Maximum length 1.73cm.

96E138:61 This portion of a flint flake was found in a very disturbed context immediately outside the curved Phase 2 façade. It is slightly weathered and patinated beige and brown. It has been fractured after being retouched into a simple scraper. Maximum length 2.2cm.

96E138:68 This comparatively fresh, small portion of a flint flake was found at the base of the cairn core. Maximum length 1.93cm.

CHERT

96E138:19 This fragment was found in the collapse from the rampart in the most northerly rampart section. It is from a nodule of glossy black chert and retains some possible flake scars. Maximum length 1.2cm.

96E138:4 This possible portion of a very weathered chert flake was found in the topsoil covering the cairn. Maximum length 1.52cm.

96E138:6 This portion of a small flake of glossy, black chert was found in the same place as no. 4 above. Maximum length 1.53cm.

96E138:12 This fractured portion of a piece of chert was found within the rampart in section 4. It is possibly, though not certainly, struck. Maximum length 1.6cm.

96E138:29 This large chert flake was found in a very disturbed context on the north side of the cairn. It splays to a broad distal end. Maximum length 4cm; maximum breadth 5.1cm.

96E138:44 This stray find was found on the western extent of the reef. It may have been struck and there is slight damage on two edges. Maximum length 1.71cm.

96E138:53 This small portion of what might have been a chert flake was found near the surface of the extant remains of the cairn core. Maximum length 1.5cm.

RHYOLITE

96E138:36 This blade of rhyolite was found in the redeposited boulder clay at the base of the very disturbed north side of the cairn. It still retains its water-smoothed outer surface and has a large, smooth striking platform. Maximum length 7.3cm; maximum breadth 1.5cm.

GREENSTONE

96 E138:11 This flake came from the general cairn material which covered the tomb. It has been struck from either a water-rolled pebble or a polished stone axe. The smoothed surface only survives at the distal end as several other flakes have been removed. Irregular peripheral retouch occurs along the distal and right lateral edges. Maximum length 2.5cm; maximum breadth 2.3cm.

Pl. 35—Stone objects.

73

LIGNITE

96E138:68 This item was found amidst the collapse of the rampart in section 3 and may be a portion of a lignite disc. The piece has two flat surfaces and retains some crude peripheral retouch on one edge, which gives the surviving section a curved shape.

COMMENT

In common with many other lithic assemblages from the south-west of Ireland, the collection from Ballycarty has a surprisingly low incidence of chert artefacts. Only two pieces, notably the large chert flake (29) and a portion of a spall of glossy black chert (6), can be stated unequivocally to have been the product of knapping. The tendency to rely on flint has already been noted by Woodman and Scannell (1993). One small difference between this assemblage and others, such as those from Lough Gur, is that no quartz artefacts were found at Ballycarty.

The small assemblage of flint artefacts would appear to have utilised either small beach-rolled nodules or small pieces of *remaniée* flint and, in common with other assemblages from the region, many of the retouched tools have been made on primary cortical flakes, e.g. the large scraper (20), or else from split pebbles.

Much of the material is heavily patinated and/or weathered, and most of the unretouched pieces are shattered fragments of larger artefacts. The bulk of the assemblage therefore has the appearance of being in a secondary or derived context or has been exposed to the elements for a significant length of time. Only two pieces, the bipolar core (14B) and the small scraper (15), are comparatively unpatinated.

There are no particularly diagnostic implements in this assemblage. The small size of the scrapers is sometimes thought to be an attribute of Bronze Age assemblages, but reduction in size can also be a product of raw material availability. The slightly invasive character of the retouch on no. 20 could, however, suggest a Bronze Age date. Similarly, no. 17 could be a portion of a slug knife of a type normally found in Bronze Age assemblages, although this is by no means a certain identification. The simple bipolar core could date from either the Neolithic or the Bronze Age. The fact that not one of the Neolithic 'type fossils' such as leaf/lozenge arrowheads, hollow scrapers or elongated plano-convex knives was recovered from the site must be given consideration.

On the basis of evidence from elsewhere on the west coast, the flint could have been derived from local beaches or remnants of flint left behind (the Gweestin Bridge downfault of cretaceous deposits containing flint lies within 20km of Ballycarty). Chert could occur locally in the area, and it is possible that the rhyolite blade was either imported or made from a nodule brought from the volcanic deposits at the western end of the Dingle Peninsula.

In contrast, the greenstone flake would be more in place in parts of east Limerick, adjacent to Lough Gur. Therefore, while much of the material found at Ballycarty could have originated in the immediate area, certain pieces must have been brought in.

APPENDIX 2. THE CREMATED REMAINS

CATRYN POWER
Department of Archaeology,
University College Cork

All archaeological contexts were examined for the presence of human remains. Human bones were positively identified in two contexts. No pathology or anomalies were evident on these small pieces of bone. Many fragments of the osteological remains from Ballycarty are unidentifiable; some of these could well be human but their fragmentary state makes this impossible to determine.

A minimum of one person is represented at Ballycarty, but it is not possible to determine whether these fragments, from two bones (the skull and the ulna), come from one or two individuals. Neither is it possible to assess the age of the individual(s); however, it can be determined that an adolescent or mature adult is represented.

The two identified fragments are 15mm in size and are white. The colour and calcined appearance indicate that they were efficiently cremated at a temperature of at least 800°C. The intensity of the heat removes all the organic matter from the bone and dehydrates the calcium and phosphate salts to an acid–insoluble form.

During the cremation process the body shrinks, and the white fragments from Ballycarty indicate as much as 25% shrinkage. Certain parts of the body survive the cremation better than others, and one such bone portion is present here (part of the petrous portion of the skull). The fact that the bones are well cremated would indicate that this practice was well established at Ballycarty.

The size of the fragments is similar to that seen in other assemblages, such as that dating from the Neolithic from the passage tomb at Knowth, Co. Meath, where the remains of at least 49 cremated individuals were found. A Bronze Age collection of cremated bone from Mounthawk, Tralee, also yielded fragments of similar size.

At Knowth the suggested reasons for the small size of the bone fragments include regular stoking of the pyre during the cremation process, which would lead to the fragmentation of the hot, brittle and heat-fractured bone. Following removal from the pyre, fragmentation of the bones would also occur during transportation to the place of burial. Another cause of fragmentation is the winnowing of the 'hot ashes' in water, to separate the debris, which included charcoal and bone fragments. This would result in a clean collection of bones.

A modern adult cremation results in between 1600g and 3600g of bone, depending on the individual. At Ballycarty only a few grammes of bone are present, and some of this may be animal; therefore most of the human bone is missing, even if only one individual is represented. This bone may have perished in the tomb, it may have been removed during the various periods of site disturbance, or it may have been buried elsewhere. Perhaps only a token of the individual was interred in the tomb.

THE CREMATED HUMAN BONE FRAGMENTS

Context B1 C28

This small fragment, from a layer of black soil in the Phase 2/3 chamber, is from the petrous portion of the mastoid process from the skull of a mature adult. The bone is white (Pl. 36).

Pl. 36—The cremated human bone—mastoid process on the left, fragment from an adult ulna on the right.

Context B3 C42

This white fragment of bone, from the base of the general cairn material on the north side of the site, is from the mid-shaft of a mature adult ulna (part of the forearm).

APPENDIX 3. THE ANIMAL BONES

MARGARET McCARTHY
Department of Archaeology,
University College Cork

The excavations at Ballycarty produced a relatively large amount of animal and bird bones, which were submitted to the Archaeological Services Unit in University College Cork for analysis. The bone material came from six main areas of investigation and the largest collections came from the cairn/tomb (area B1) and the interface of rampart, cairn and court (area C3). Bones from one of the rampart sections (area C2) were not examined as they appeared to be residual in nature and the butchery was sometimes modern in character.

In general the soil conditions at the site were not conducive to the preservation of organic material. The ratios of loose teeth to identified bone fragments are often a useful indicator of bone survival—the higher the ratio, the poorer bone survival is likely to have been. The ratios calculated for the different phases at Ballycarty confirm the overall poor survival conditions at the site, and the analysis and interpretation of the assemblage are undertaken with the assumption that differential preservation of bones from animals and birds of different sizes and ages will have distorted the bone record.

Only 8% of the fragments had any surviving articulations and the sample was dominated by fragments with good survival potential, particularly loose teeth and upper limb bone fragments. Owing to these adverse preservation conditions there were insufficient data to generalise about age structures and kill patterns, and the sample of measurable bone was negligible.

It was clear from the incidence of canid gnawing on the bones that dogs played a significant role in the degeneration of the faunal samples, and this placed limits upon the degree to which cut-marks and pathological variations could be observed.

There were large numbers of charred and calcined bones throughout the various phases and contexts, and those from the passageway of the megalith and the rock-cut pits in the forecourt area showed the highest degree of burning. Many of these fragments were examined as possible cremated human remains, but they proved too small to permit any convincing distinction between human and animal bones.

RECOVERY

Information on bone material came from two sources—from bulk collection in the trenches and from samples of soil taken from various contexts. The large domestic animals formed the bulk of the assemblage, and no fish bones were recovered despite a programme of sieving. In general, the sieved samples proved very unproductive in terms of bone recovery and, apart from establishing the presence of pygmy shrew at the site, no other material of osteological significance was noted.

METHODS

The bone material was compared with modern reference collections in the Department of

Archaeology, University College Cork. The bones were recorded by area and studied according to the contexts in which they were found. Data were recorded using a computer-coded scheme designed specifically for faunal analysis, which includes categories for recording not only species and age profiles but also erosion, butchery and fragmentation. All raw data are stored in the Archaeological Services Unit and may be obtained from there on request.

Identifications were taken to species where possible; otherwise wider categories were used. For example, when a bone could not be assigned with certainty to pig or sheep the category 'medium mammal' (MM in Fig. 23) was used. In the same way, bones that could not definitely be recorded as cattle were classed as 'large mammal' (LM in Fig. 23). The ovicaprid bones are all referred to as sheep in the text, as many of them bore anatomical features reliably distinguishing them to that species and there were no diagnostic goat bones.

The relative abundance of the animals present was expressed in terms of the total number of identifiable bones and, in a few instances, by estimating the minimum number of individuals present.

	Horse	Cattle	Sheep	Pig	Dog	Rodent	Rabbit	Bird	LM*	MM*	UNID*	TOTALS
Cairn & tomb												
Phase 1	1	8	5	-	-	2	-	1	17	5	27	66
Phase 2	-	4	1	1	2	2	-	4	3	-	3	20
Phase 3	5	22	24	13	122	1	-	85	26	99	394	791
North side of forecourt	-	17	14	7	2	-	-	-	50	46	67	203
North side of cairn	2	43	15	11	-	-	2	1	85	95	128	382
Forecourt												
Phase 2	-	18	12	8	-	-	-	1	27	52	71	189
Phase 3	-	3	-	3	2	-	-	1	7	1	51	68
Rampart	-	20	5	12	-	-	27	-	43	27	137	271
Rampart sections	-	3	-	-	-	-	-	-	8	-	-	11
TOTALS	8	138	76	55	128	5	29	93	266	325	878	2001

LM* Large mammal   MM* Medium mammal   Unid* Unidentifiable specimen

Fig. 23—Table showing the range, location and phasing of the animal remains.

ANALYSIS

A total of 2001 bone and tooth fragments were examined, originating mostly from the cairn and tomb (44%) and the court and rampart area in front of the tomb (26%). The assemblage was extremely fragmented and just 27% of the bones were diagnostic to species. The remainder of the material was ascribed to one of the categories mentioned above, and 44% were tiny unidentifiable fragments, many of which were totally calcined. Figure 23 lists the identified species found by normal hand recovery from all excavated areas, and the results of the analysis are summarised below by area and phase.

THE CAIRN AND MEGALITHIC TOMB

This was one of the main areas of work at the site, and a total of 877 fragments, including 93 bird bones, were recovered from the three phases of megalithic construction recognised by the excavator.

Phase 1
In all, 64 bones were recovered from deposits and layers associated with the primary construction phase of the monument. The material originated mostly from surface spreads between the large chamber and the middle ring of stone; two bird claws were recovered from C17, a post-hole within the chamber, and the excavator has interpreted these as a ritual deposit.

Preservation was poor and a large number of eroded fragments and loose teeth were recovered. Unidentifiable material formed a very high proportion of the assemblage (42%) and only fifteen animal bones were diagnostic to species. Cattle (8) fragments slightly outnumbered those of sheep (5), and there was no evidence of pig. The distal end of a cattle humerus was chopped axially and came from an animal at least one and a half years of age at slaughter. The most interesting specimen from this phase was a single horse tooth from a charcoal-flecked layer within the chamber. Another find which deserves special mention is the identification of two limb bones of a pygmy shrew (*Sorex minutus*) from the basal layer of soil on the site. The pygmy shrew is Ireland's smallest native mammalian species and, to the author's knowledge, this is the first recorded instance from an archaeological site.

The remainder of the mammalian remains consisted of seventeen fragments of bone from larger animals and five fragments from smaller animals which were too badly broken to be further identified. There was just one bird bone from this phase, identified as the proximal end of a femur of a song-thrush (*Turdus philomelos*). The bone was recovered from a reddish brown layer with charcoal and burnt stones, located between the chamber and the middle ring of stones.

Phase 2
Only a few fragments of poorly preserved bone were recovered from deposits associated with the construction of the secondary passage, chamber and façade. The samples (20 specimens) were recovered from two deposits within the chamber and little can be said about them, except that as well as documenting the occurrence of the three main domestic species, the remains of dog and woodmouse (*Apodemus sylvaticus*) were also included.

Dog was represented by a complete second phalanx and the fused distal portion of a tibia. The latter bone had a distal breadth (Bd) of 20.1mm and belonged to a relatively large, Labrador-sized dog. The distal lateral portion of sheep metatarsus was fused, which indicated that the animal was older than two years at slaughter. Four bird bones were recovered from C41 and these were identified as redwing (*Turdus iliacus*), the smallest of the common thrushes in Ireland.

Phase 3

A total of 126 bones were recovered from deposits associated with the final phase of activity at the site. The material originated from a variety of features, including a pit and various fills of the Phase 3 passage.

A small circular pit in the passage produced the totally calcined remains of a humerus from a sheep-sized animal and five unidentifiable longbone fragments. A black soil which filled the upper levels of the passage and sealed the remains of the chamber produced an interesting collection of four dog bones (three teeth and the proximal mid-shaft portion of an ulna), a woodmouse skull and the remains of at least two corncrakes (*Crex crex*). A slightly oxidised deposit within the passage yielded a total sample of seventeen bones, and cattle (2), sheep (2) and pig (1) were all represented (Fig. 23).

The cairn

The cairn contributed by far the largest sample to the assemblage. In all, 665 bone fragments were examined. Preservation was reasonably good and this resulted in a fairly even distribution of the different bone elements. The remains listed as unidentifiable in Fig. 23 are nearly all from the cairn and are mostly small crumbs of bones from ungulates.

An extensive deposit of cairn material produced the largest sample of bones and also the greatest range of mammalian and avian species for the site. This context alone provided over 36% of the total faunal assemblage. Most common in the sample were bones of the three major livestock animals, cattle, sheep and pig. Sheep (24) were slightly more common than cattle (22), and pig (13) ranked a close third. The majority of the sheep bones came from the upper right forelimb, and at least three individuals were recognised. The ages represented varied, with some lamb and foetal limb bones and some large mature fragments. There were no sheep jaws with ageing data, but all the loose molars were in an advanced stage of wear.

Ageing data from cattle limb bones showed a similar pattern of age distribution to sheep, with two juvenile metapodial fragments and phalanges from individuals over one and a half years. The pig assemblage was dominated by loose teeth and fragments of upper limb bones, including the proximal epiphysis of a tibia.

Butchery marks were noted on the cattle bones and consisted mainly of heavy chop-marks on the major limbs. Two vertebrae provided evidence for the lateral division of the carcass and it is likely that superficial knife-marks have been obscured as a result of the overall poor condition of the material.

Other species represented were horse and dog and there was no evidence for the exploitation of wild species, apart from the recovery of a small perforated antler disc. The group of five horse teeth were not especially worn or immature and probably came from individuals aged 6–8 years. An almost complete skeleton of an adult, probably female, dog of sheepdog size was recovered from the lowest levels of the cairn. Despite the fragmentary nature of the collection, no butchery marks were found on the bones and it can be inferred that the animal was buried whole. The remains included the skull, most of the vertebrae (all epiphyses fused), ribs, fragments of the forelimbs and hind limbs, phalanges and a complete calcaneum, which measured 39.8mm in length. The only other mammal species present in the cairn deposits was woodmouse, which is probably intrusive.

Excavations on the northern side of the cairn yielded a total sample of 382 poorly preserved bones. The mammalian species present were cattle, sheep, pig and horse. Cattle was the dominant species, contributing 43 fragments to a total of 72 identifiable bones. The cattle sample contained a high proportion of limb bone fragments, as well as loose teeth, vertebrae and the proximal end of a calf tibia. All fifteen sheep fragments belonged to the skull, scapula and upper limb bones. The eleven fragments identified as pig consisted mostly of loose teeth and limb bone fragments. Butchery marks were identified on eight cattle bones and these indicated that the carcasses had been disarticulated and stripped of meat before disposal.

A very small proportion of horse was present, comprising two heavily worn molars from the cairn deposits. Two juvenile rabbit bones from these deposits were probably a later contaminant, as this species was not introduced into Ireland until the thirteenth century. Also present in this layer was the proximal portion of the humerus of a barn owl (*Tyto alba*). Barn owls usually inhabit open, arid countryside with scattered trees, and feed mainly on small rodents.

The bird bones
Bird bones made a major contribution to the totals for Phase 3 and the cairn deposits. The following species were identified:

Corncrake (*Crex crex*)
Snipe (*Gallinago gallinago*)
Bar-tailed godwit (*Limosa lapponica*)
Robin (*Erithacus rubecula*)
Redwing (*Turdus iliacus*)
Song-thrush (*Turdus philomelos*)

Corncrakes were the most common bird identified, representing 42% of the total avian assemblage and occurring exclusively within the Phase 2/3 passage. This species was present as two partial skeletons, with wing bones predominating. Song-thrush was the second most commonly represented bird, and 29 bones, from at least three individuals, were recovered from the cairn.

In interpreting the assemblage of wild birds, it is useful to consider them in ecological groups. Many of the species from Ballycarty frequent wooded and estuarine environments and a number of common garden species are also present. Corncrakes are indicators of both dry and moist meadows and were probably quite common in the region in the past. Snipe and godwits breed in marshes, bogs and damp meadows, and their presence at the site is indicative of nearby areas of woodland and wet marshy land. Redwings nest in forested (especially birch) areas, and the two other species identified from the site, song-thrush and robin, also frequent forests, scrub and hedgerows.

THE NORTH SIDE OF THE FORECOURT

The animal bone from this area was relatively small in quantity and was in an eroded and weathered condition. In all, 203 fragments were recovered, the majority from various deposits and layers associated with the construction of the rampart.

A very small sample of five bones was recovered from a deposit within a large rock-cut pit. The only identifiable bone was an extremely worn sheep incisor, and the remainder were classified as large and medium mammal fragments. Cattle (17) and sheep (14) dominated the identifiable assemblage, and pig bones (7) were once again found in smaller quantities. A single adult dog was represented by the fused proximal and distal portions of a tibia.

Preservation in this area was generally very poor, and 61% of the fragments were eroded and weathered. No partial or complete skeletons were recovered and the sample was considered too small for further analysis.

THE FORECOURT, CAIRN/RAMPART INTERFACE AND RAMPART SECTIONS

Faunal material from this area was recovered in small amounts from layers and deposits relating to Phases 2 and 3 of the megalithic tomb and in larger amounts from deposits relating to the rampart.

Phase 2

A total of 189 bones were recovered from contexts associated with Phase 2 of the megalithic tomb, and these consisted mostly of unidentifiable remains (71) and fragments of large mammal (27) and medium mammal (52) longbones. The three main domestic species—cattle, sheep and pig—were present, in ascending order of frequency. A single coracoid bone, identified as barn owl, and two molars from an adult dog were recovered from a pit cut into the natural bedrock.

Phase 3

The samples from Phase 3 contexts were very small and only a few comments are in order. The deposits produced some 68 fragments of bone, only nine of which were identifiable. Cattle and pig were represented by three cranial fragments each, and there was no evidence for sheep. A cattle mandible was severely eroded and none of the teeth survived in sockets. Two pig molars were worn and belonged to individuals over two years of age.

Little else can be said about the sample except that it included the proximal portion of a tarso–metatarsus of a song-thrush. It was also noticeable that this particular collection of bones had the highest rate of unidentifiability (75%) for all phases at the site.

The rampart

A total of 271 bones were recovered from deposits associated with the rampart sections. Most of the bones were either specific to domestic species or to small fragments derived from them. Cattle (20) and pig (12) contributed the greatest number of bones to the identifiable sample. Of the three main livestock animals, sheep (5) occurred least frequently in terms of identifiable fragments, but the presence of at least two individuals was established from proximal tibiae. Ageing data were scarce, but the results indicated that all cattle had reached adulthood before slaughter. Among the pig bones was an unfused phalanx from an individual less than one year old, and the three sheep molars were from mature animals.

The sample of identifiable bones from the rampart was dominated by rabbit (27). It is always difficult to decide whether rabbit remains are contemporary with a deposit. In this instance it is unlikely that the bones are associated with the original use of the rampart, as the presence of two partial skeletons, one of which was immature, suggests that the animals may have burrowed into the rampart. The absence of butchery marks, together with the very fresh state of the bones in comparison to the other material, adds support to this interpretation.

CONCLUSIONS

The faunal material from the megalithic tomb at Ballycarty was recovered from all areas of the site and it is difficult to link the bones to ritual practices. Apart from a few possible ritual deposits in the rock-cut pits and the passageway, there were no traces of specialised treatment or disposal of ungulate carcasses or bones.

The bulk of the material appears to have been discarded in a relatively unspecialised manner during the various phases of construction of the tomb. The assemblage represents a selection of both meat-bearing and peripheral parts of the skeleton, and some of these bore cut-marks associated with jointing and meat removal.

The indications are therefore that these skeletal elements were the product of food refuse, discarded by the builders of the monument. Most of the identifiable bones were either specific to domestic cattle and sheep or small fragments probably derived from them. The distribution of carcass components suggested that primary butchery was being practised either at the site or very close by.

Differential preservation appears to have been a significant factor in the formation of the faunal samples examined, and the soil conditions seem to have favoured the survival of large mammal bones. Loose teeth and the mid-shaft portions of dense upper limb bones were found in abundance, and the percentage of longbones with surviving articulations was low for the three main livestock animals.

Other animal species were present in very small quantities. Of note was the recovery of the remains of a pygmy shrew from the primary construction of the monument, and the claws of a large bird from the same post-hole. The bones of woodmouse were recovered from the two later structural phases, and one theory for the presence of these rodents is that they were introduced by birds.

The density of bones recovered from the cairn was quite high and included the almost complete skeleton of a dog. There were eight horse teeth from the whole site and, with the exception of a single molar from a Phase 1 deposit, they were all associated with the third phase of activity at the site. The presence of horse in the primary construction phase is perhaps the most interesting aspect of the assemblage, given the potentially early date for the monument.

Corncrakes and thrushes formed a relatively large proportion of the avifauna and the presence of corncrake is one more illustration of the former wide distribution of a bird that now breeds in very small numbers in Ireland. In general, the sample of bird bones was very useful as an indicator of the local environment and, with the exception of the corncrake, all these species may be found in nearby wooded areas and marshlands at the present day.

In conclusion, the features that stand out from the examination of the faunal material from Ballycarty are the rather high proportion of wild bird species, the occurrence of a horse bone in a possible early prehistoric context, and the recovery of pygmy shrew bones from a post-hole inside the primary chamber. To the best of the author's knowledge, the pygmy shrew from Ballycarty seems to be the first recorded find of this species from an Irish archaeological site.

APPENDIX 4. ARCHAEOBOTANICAL EVALUATION REPORT

JOHN TIERNEY
Eachtra Archaeological Projects

The purpose of this project was to assess the ecofactual content of ten samples from the excavations at Ballycarty. All samples were sieved using a combination of flotation and washover. The flot material was captured in sieves with mesh sizes of 1mm, 500μm and 300μm. Once dried, the flots were examined under a zoom-lensed stereo microscope, and their ecofactual content noted on a semi-quantitive basis.

Sample 1
Charcoal-rich deposit from north side of forecourt. Charcoal fragments and occasional molluscs. Moderate amounts of modern twigs. One possible piece of bone. Approximately 18 cereal fragments and whole grains.

Sample 2
Burnt deposit from large rock-cut, slag-filled pit. Three medium-sized bone fragments and 30 cereal fragments.

Sample 3
Grey ash deposit inside entrance of Phase 3 passage. Occasional molluscs, many rooty materials. Occasional poorly preserved bone and abundant charcoal. Approximately 40 cereal grains and fragments.

Sample 4
Charcoal-stained layer from north side of forecourt. Charcoal abundant. No molluscs, no bone, a few twigs.

Sample 5
Burnt basal layer of boulder clay inside Phase 1 chamber. Occasional bark fragments. Moderate amount of root and twig fragments. Occasional land molluscs. Approximately 40 cereal grains.

Sample 6
Burnt layer from north side of forecourt. Abundant charcoal fragments and twigs. Between 30 and 40 charred cereal grains.

Sample 7
Fill of post-hole inside Phase 1 chamber. One *Plantago lanceolata* and occasional other weeds. Occasional molluscs and bark pieces. Abundant twigs and roots. Frequent small limb bones (pygmy shrew). Abundant poorly preserved cereal grains.

Sample 8
Grey ash deposit in forecourt. Abundant twig fragments. Occasional charcoal fragments. Occasional modern beetle fragments. Approximately 40 cereal fragments and whole grains.

Sample 9
Upper fill of Phase 2/3 chamber. Abundance of twig fragments. Occasional molluscs and approximately 20 cereal grains.

Sample 10
Lower fill of Phase 2/3 chamber. Occasional fragments of root. Occasional large molluscs. Frequent weed seeds and approximately 15 cereal grains.

CONCLUSIONS

Nine out of ten samples produced plant remains, both cereal grains and weeds. The relatively high quantities of plant remains found and the variety of cereal types and weeds present are indicative of domestic debris. The good preservational condition of the seeds, with the exception of those from the post-hole inside the primary chamber (Sample 7), is indicative of more recently deposited remains.

APPENDIX 5. THE GEOLOGY AND PALAEONTOLOGY OF THE PASSAGE TOMB, WITH COMMENTS ON THE SIGNIFICANCE OF THE FOSSILS AND GEOLOGICAL FINDS

PATRICK N. WYSE JACKSON
Department of Geology,
Trinity College Dublin

INTRODUCTION

Ballycarty passage tomb is situated on the western side of a low hill three miles east of Tralee, 50m south of the River Lee, in the townland of Ballycarty. On excavation numerous loose fossils were recovered both in the cairn fill and within the primary chamber itself. The fossils and other geological specimens are the subject of this report.

GEOLOGICAL SETTING

The area between Tralee and Castleisland to the east (the Vale of Tralee) and the Magherees and Camp on the Dingle Peninsula to the west is underlain by a succession of limestones and shales that were deposited during the Lower Carboniferous. This narrow strip of low-lying terrain is sandwiched between areas of considerable topographical relief to the north-east and to the south. Older sediments, including the Old Red Sandstone of Devonian age, which forms the bulk of the Slieve Mish Mountains, are exposed to the south, while to the north-east younger black shales that were deposited during the Upper Carboniferous form the Stacks Mountains.

Ballycarty is underlain by Waulsortian Limestone of Early Carboniferous age, which in the Tralee area reaches 600m in thickness (Thornton 1966). Within this unit occurs limestone of two differing styles. At the base of the unit are the well-bedded limestones (the Castleisland Limestones of Hudson *et al.* 1966), which are pale grey in colour, partially dolomitised in parts and highly fossiliferous, with corals, goniatites, nautiloids and brachiopods (Hudson *et al.* 1966). These bedded limestones grade or interdigitate with developments of unbedded, massive, pale grey limestones which formed discrete banks of aggregated lime mud, known as Waulsortian mudmounds.

Waulsortian mudmounds are found in western Europe, North America and Asia (Lees and Miller 1995). In Ireland they were most extensively developed (Sevastopulo 1982). They grew from the seabed through the accumulation of limey mud and developed relief up to 200m. Waulsortian mudmounds occurred individually where they reached a thickness of several tens of metres and an area of several hundreds of metres, or as large banks where several coalesced, with thicknesses of 1km and an areal extent of 30,000 square kilometres.

Waulsortian limestone contains abundant and diverse fossil assemblages, the distribution of which is often depth-determined: bryozoans and crinoids are most common in basal portions, while Foraminifera and algae are found in upper portions. Bryozoans, brachiopods, cephalopods and gastropods are common, while corals are rare.

GEOLOGY OF THE BALLYCARTY PASSAGE TOMB

At Ballycarty, a Waulsortian mudmound now forms a hill 32m high, on which the passage tomb is located. The tomb is constructed of Waulsortian limestone which was collected from the immediate area. Natural joints, which trend broadly east–west, developed in the limestone, allowing the builders of the tomb to extract largish blocks without having to break or work the stone. The boulders are irregular to regular in shape, and average 75cm in length, width and height. The natural flat joint surfaces of the boulders have been aligned to form the smooth walls of the passage and chamber.

GEOLOGICAL FINDS IN THE TOMB

Within the primary chamber and in the cairn infill a variety of geological objects were recovered and these have been examined. Although the bulk of the material consisted of various Carboniferous fossils, some other cobbles, nodules and limestone fragments are of interest. Brief descriptive notes are given below.

FOSSILS

These are all derived from the Waulsortian limestone and were probably collected on the site or close by. Most of the fossils have a slightly roughened texture, indicating that they were exposed on the surface for some time. This, together with the development of soil, generally loosens the fossils from the surrounding rock matrix, which would have made it relatively easy for the builders of the passage grave to winkle out complete or nearly complete specimens. Only one, *Naticopsis*, a large gastropod, shows some fresh broken surfaces, which may have been where matrix was broken away by the collector.

Brachiopoda

Productoids: *Eomarginifera* sp. (one specimen), *Productus* sp. (two specimens).

Spirifids: *Brachythris pinguis* (one specimen, Pl. 37.8), *Martina glabra* (one specimen, Pl. 37.7), *Spirifer coplowensis* (five specimens, Pl. 37.9).

Terebratulids: *Dielasma hastatum* (one specimen, Pl. 37.6).

Cephalopoda

Orthoconic nautiloids (straight-shelled): *Kionoceras* sp. (one specimen), orthoconic nautiloid spp indet. (two specimens, Pl. 37.4).

Cyrtoconic nautiloids (curved-shelled): *Eusthenoceras* sp. (one specimen).

Coiled nautiloids (coiled-shelled): *Epidomatoceras* sp. (one specimen), *Maccoyceras* sp. (one specimen), *Subvestinautilus crateriformis* (two specimens, Pl. 37.3), coiled nautiloid sp. indet. (one specimen).

Gonitiates: *Gonitiates* sp. (one specimen, Pl. 37.5).

Gastropoda

Euomphalus pentangulatus (one complete specimen, nine fragments, Pl. 37.1).
Naticopsis sp. (one specimen).
Flemingia prisca (one specimen, Pl. 37.2).

Crinoidea (sea lilies)

Crinoid stems indet.

NON-FOSSILIFEROUS MATERIAL

Six specimens, most of which were derived locally, were found.

Two rounded cobbles of Old Red Sandstone (91mm and 77mm in max. diameter) from the Slieve Mish Mountains. These were two examples of broken cobbles which were recovered in great numbers from the cairn fill and from inside the tomb. They were derived from local glacial till that covers much of the area. Both have been broken in half, which may have happened if they were used as hand-tools or were subjected to heat.

Carboniferous limestone bead (96E138:55) with small rectangular depressions produced by marine boring sponges and a slightly larger man-made hole at one end. Similar limestone found on present-day beaches around Tralee is commonly bored by sponges, and it is therefore most likely that the bead was collected from a local beach.

Black chert fragment (33mm in diameter) derived from local Carboniferous limestone.

Quartz crystal (20mm across), one of many recovered from the site.

Rounded ironstone nodule (29mm by 15mm) derived from Upper Carboniferous rocks (probably from the north-east).

Siltstone fragment (21mm across) of unknown origin.

SIGNIFICANCE OF THE FOSSILS

Fossils are the remains of plants and animals that are preserved in rock. For many millennia fossils have been objects of curiosity, but only in the last 150 years have they been systematically studied and described.

It is thought that by the sixth century BC the Greeks had worked out the connection between fossils and living organisms, and it is probable that the Chinese had done likewise. When Pythagoras noticed shells in mountain rocks he deduced that the mountains must have been below sea-level at some time in the past. Pliny the Elder, who lived between 23 and 79 BC, noted several fossils, including shells and sponges, in his writings, and correctly attributed amber to pine trees.

Throughout medieval times it appears that the true nature of fossils was unknown to researchers, and legends and folklore grew up about various fossils (Bassett 1982; Oakley 1965; Zammit Maempel 1989). In popular folklore many fossils were given names that alluded to their supposed origins. In England, pointed shells of the cephalopod *Belemnites* were thought to be petrified thunderbolts, on account of their shape; the bivalve *Gryphaea arcuata*, commonly found in rocks around the River Severn, was called the Devil's Toenail; the echinoid *Micraster* has a heart-shaped shell which was known to local people on the south coast of England as a fairy loaf, and crinoid stems were known as screwstones.

There have been few examples of fossils being used by early man for decoration and

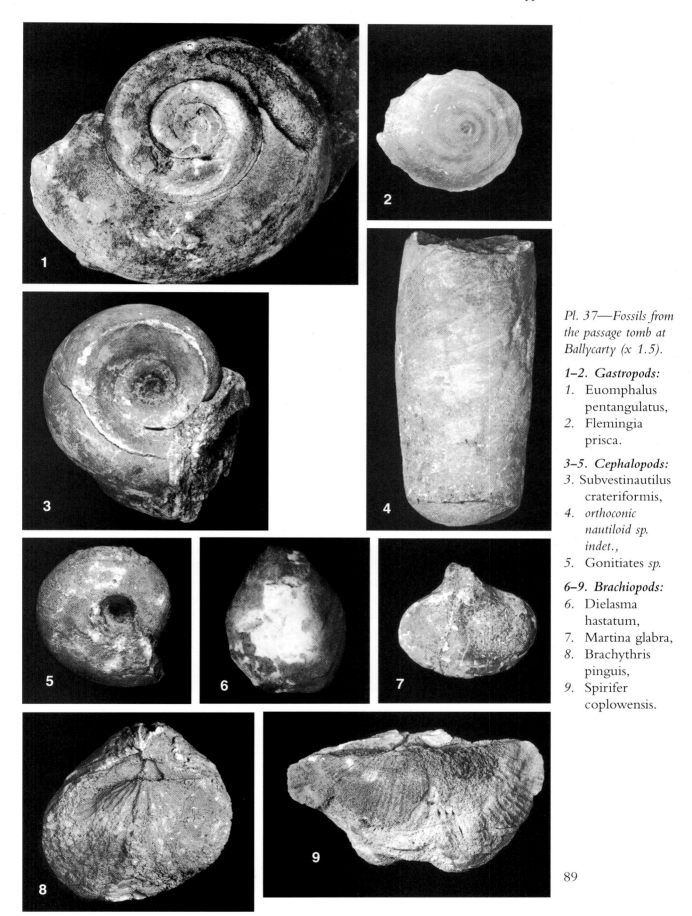

Pl. 37—Fossils from the passage tomb at Ballycarty (x 1.5).

1–2. Gastropods:
1. Euomphalus pentangulatus,
2. Flemingia prisca.

3–5. Cephalopods:
3. Subvestinautilus crateriformis,
4. orthoconic nautiloid sp. indet.,
5. Gonitiates *sp.*

6–9. Brachiopods:
6. Dielasma hastatum,
7. Martina glabra,
8. Brachythris pinguis,
9. Spirifer coplowensis.

adornment. Fossils have been reported from a number of Upper Palaeolithic and later sites in Europe and North America, where they were used for necklaces and pendants, or for decorative purposes (Oakley 1965). Necklaces of Tertiary fossils have been recovered from the Upper Palaeolithic burial site at Dolni Vestonice, Moravia; of the small, bead-like sponge *Porosphaera* from the Bronze Age site at Higham Marshes, near Gravesend, England; and of the trilobite *Elrathia kingii* from early nineteenth-century Indian sites in Utah, USA (Bassett 1982; Taylor and Robison 1976).

Until now, the earliest recorded occurrences of fossils used for ceremonial purposes in burials were those from the early Bronze Age tumulus on the Dunstable Downs, near the south coast of England, and from Stonepark, near Claremorris, Co. Mayo. At the former site nearly 100 Chalk fossil sea-urchins surrounding the remains of a woman and child have been interpreted as having a ceremonial significance (Oakley 1965; Smith 1894). Alternatively, perhaps, the fossils may have been thought to have constituted a source of food which could be used by the deceased in any future incarnation. In the 1930s, when a cist grave at Stonepark was excavated, a specimen of the Carboniferous coral *Michelina megastoma* was discovered, and was thought to have been worn as an amulet (Langan 1934).

In megalithic tombs in Ireland beads, pottery, stone pendants and stone balls have been commonly found. It is thought that the latter may have been fertility symbols (Ó Nualláin 1991). Uniquely at Ballycarty loose fossils have been discovered within a passage tomb which would appear to significantly pre-date the examples on Dunstable Downs and in County Mayo.

It is not possible that these fossils could have become incorporated into the passage tomb at Ballycarty through natural erosion processes. Rather, they were collected purposely by the builders of the tomb and placed within it. What these early builders made of the fossils is impossible to say, but they clearly recognised their unique features and considered them interesting and valuable. It is probable that the fossils were placed with the remains of the dead as ceremonial decorations, ornaments or charms.

CONCLUSIONS

A diverse assemblage of Lower Carboniferous fossils discovered in a megalithic passage tomb at Ballycarty, Co. Kerry, is considered to be the first such find in Ireland. The fossils, which include brachiopods, gastropods and cephalopods, were collected from the immediate area and placed within the tomb by the builders, probably for some ceremonial or decorative purpose. The occurrence of fossils in the passage tomb at Ballycarty pre-dates similar instances in Bronze Age burial chambers.

ACKNOWLEDGEMENTS

Plate 37 was prepared by Declan Burke, Department of Geology, Trinity College Dublin.

REFERENCES

Bassett, M.G. 1982 *Formed stones—folklore and fossils.* National Museum of Wales Geological Series 1.

Hudson, R.G.S., Clarke, M.J. and Brennand, P.T. 1966 The Lower Carboniferous

(Dinantian) stratigraphy of the Castleisland area, Co. Kerry. *Scientific Proceedings of the Royal Dublin Society*, Series A, **2**, 297–317.

Langan, S. 1934 Discovery of cists. *Journal of the Galway Archaeological and Historical Society* **16**, 57–61.

Lees, A. and Miller, J. 1995 Waulsortian banks. In C.L.V. Monty, D.W.J. Bosence, P.H. Bridges and B.R. Pratt, *Carbonate mud-mounds: their origin and evolution*, 191–271. International Association of Sedimentologists Special Publication No. 23. Oxford. Blackwell.

Oakley, K.P. 1965 Folklore of fossils. *Antiquity* **39**, 9–16, 117–25.

Ó Nualláin, S. 1991 The megalithic tomb builders. In M. Ryan (ed.), *The illustrated archaeology of Ireland*, 55–9. Dublin. Country House.

Sevastopulo, G.D. 1982 The age and setting of Waulsortian limestones in Ireland. In K. Bolton, H.R. Lane and D.V. LeMone (eds), *Symposium on the environmental setting and distribution of the Waulsortian facies*, 65–79. El Paso. Geological Survey and University of Texas.

Smith, W.G. 1894 *Man, the primeval savage*. London.

Taylor, M.E. and Robison, R.A. 1976 Trilobites in Utah folklore. *Brigham Young University Geology Studies* **23**, 1–5.

Thornton, M.S. 1966 The Lower Carboniferous limestones of the Tralee Bay area, Co. Kerry, Ireland. Unpublished Ph.D. thesis, Cambridge University.

Zammit Maempel, G. 1989 The folklore of Maltese fossils. *Papers in Mediterranean Social Studies* **1**, 1–29.

APPENDIX 6. RADIOCARBON DETERMINATIONS

Six samples were sent for radiocarbon dating. Four were dated by conventional methods at Queen's University, Belfast, while the remaining two were accelerated dates undertaken at Oxford University.

The Queen's University samples were calibrated using 2 Sigma, giving a dating range of 95% confidence, while the Oxford samples were calibrated using the Oxcal computer program of C. Bronk Ramsey and the 1986 bi-decadal calibration curve, giving a 95.45% confidence rating.

Sample 1

UB-4165; 1450 ± 33 BP; AD 547–655.

This sample was taken from a charcoal-rich layer which overlay the Phase 2/3 chamber.

Sample 2

UB-4166; 1331 ± 39 BP; AD 641–773.

This sample was taken from the slag- and ash-filled pit near the northern side of the cairn.

Sample 3

UB-4167; 1992 ± 33 BP; 96 BC–AD 75.

This sample was taken from a very rich charcoal deposit just inside the entrance to the Phase 3 passage.

Sample 4

UB-4168; 706 ± 50 BP; AD 1257–1379.

This sample was taken from a small charcoal deposit in the redeposited boulder clay which partially filled the primary passage.

Sample 5

OxA-7530; 925 ± 45 BP; AD 1020–1210.

This sample was taken from a tiny fragment of bone found in the boulder clay at the base of the Phase 2/3 chamber.

Sample 6

OxA-7598; 740 ± 35 BP; AD 1220–1290.

This sample was taken from a small charcoal deposit within the boulder clay between the kerb and the middle ring of stone on the southern side of the site.

BIBLIOGRAPHY

Almagro, M. and Arribas, A. 1963 *El poblado y la necropolis megaliticos de los Millares.* Bibliotheca Praehistoria Hispana III. Madrid.

Barrett, J. 1988 The living, the dead and the ancestors: Neolithic and Early Bronze Age mortuary practices. In J. Barrett and I. Kinnes (eds), *The archaeology of context in the Neolithic and Early Bronze Age: recent trends,* 30–41. Sheffield University Department of Archaeology and Prehistory.

Bergh, S. 1995 *Landscape of the Monuments. A study of the passage tombs in the Cuil Irra region, Co. Sligo, Ireland.* Arkeologiska undersokningar. Skrifter nr 6. Stockholm.

Bradley, R. 1996 Excavations at Clava. *Current Archaeology* **148**, 136–42.

Bradley, R. 1998 Stone circles and passage graves—a contested relationship. In A. Gibson and D. Simpson (eds), *Prehistoric ritual and religion—essays in honour of Aubrey Burl,* 2-13. Bridgend. Sutton Publishing.

Burenhult, G. 1980a *The archaeological excavation at Carrowmore, Co. Sligo, Ireland, 1977–79.* Theses and Papers in North European Archaeology No. 9. Stockholm.

Burenhult, G. 1980b *The Carrowmore excavations. Excavation season 1980.* Stockholm Archaeological Reports No. 7.

Burenhult, G. 1981 *The Carrowmore excavations. Excavation season 1981.* Stockholm Archaeological Reports No. 8.

Burenhult, G. 1984 *The archaeology of Carrowmore.* Theses and Papers in North European Archaeology No.14. Stockholm.

Coffey, G. 1898 On a cairn excavated by Thomas Plunkett on Belmore Mountain, Co. Fermanagh. *Proceedings of the Royal Irish Academy* **20**, 259–66.

Collins, A.E.P. and Waterman, D.M. 1955 *Millin Bay, Co. Down.* Belfast. HMSO.

Collins, A.E.P. and Wilson, B.C.S. 1963 The Slieve Gullion cairns. *Ulster Journal of Archaeology* **26**, 19–40.

Condit, T. 1993 Ritual enclosures near Boyle, Co. Roscommon. *Archaeology Ireland* **7** (1), 14–16.

Condit, T. and Connolly, M. 1998 Ritual enclosures in the Lee Valley, Tralee, Co. Kerry. *Archaeology Ireland* **12** (4), 46.

Condit, T. and Simpson, D. 1998 Irish hengiform enclosures and related monuments. In A. Gibson and D. Simpson (eds), *Prehistoric ritual and religion—essays in honour of Aubrey Burl,* 45–61. Bridgend. Sutton Publishing.

Connolly, M. 1996 The passage tomb of Tralee. *Archaeology Ireland* **10** (4), 15–17.

Connolly, M. 1997 Excavations at Ballycarty, Co. Kerry. In I. Bennett (ed.), *Excavations 1996,* 46–7. Bray. Wordwell.

Connolly, M. 1997 A pilot archaeological survey of the Lee Valley, Tralee, Co. Kerry. Unpublished survey results.

Connolly, M. 1998 Copper axes and ringbarrows—ritual deposition or coincidence? *Archaeology Ireland* **12** (2), 8–10.

Connolly, M. (forthcoming) The earthen barrows of the Lee Valley, Tralee, Co. Kerry. *Journal of the Kerry Archaeological and Historical Society.*

Conwell, E.A. 1866 On ancient sepulchral cairns on the Loughcrew Hills. *Proceedings of the Royal Irish Academy* **9**, 355–79.

Cotter, C. 1995 Excavations at Dun Aonghasa, 1993. *Discovery Programme Reports. Project Results 1993,* 1–14. Dublin. Royal Irish Academy.

Cotter, C. 1996 Western Stone Fort Project. Interim report. *Discovery Programme Reports. Project Results 1994,* 1–14. Dublin. Royal Irish Academy.

Cuppage, J. 1986 *Dingle Peninsula Archaeological Survey*. Ballyferriter. Oidhreacht Corcu Dhuibhne.

Daniel, G. and Kjaerum, P. (eds) 1973 *Megalithic graves and ritual: papers presented at the third Atlantic Colloquium*. Jutland Archaeological Society Publication XI. Moesgard.

Davidson, J.L. and Henshall, A.S. 1991 *The chambered cairns of Caithness*. Edinburgh University Press.

De Valera, R. and Ó Nualláin, S. 1961 *Survey of the megalithic tombs of Ireland, Vol. I*. Dublin. Stationery Office.

De Valera, R. and Ó Nualláin, S. 1964 *Survey of the megalithic tombs of Ireland, Vol. II*. Dublin. Stationery Office.

De Valera, R. and Ó Nualláin, S. 1972 *Survey of the megalithic tombs of Ireland, Vol. III*. Dublin. Stationery Office.

De Valera, R. and Ó Nualláin, S. 1982 *Survey of the megalithic tombs of Ireland, Vol. IV*. Dublin. Stationery Office.

Dunne, L. 1998 Late Bronze Age burials in Co. Kerry. *Archaeology Ireland* **12** (2), 4.

Eogan, G. 1963 A Neolithic habitation site and megalithic tomb in Townley Hall Townland, Co. Louth. *Journal of the Royal Society of Antiquaries of Ireland* **93**, 37–81.

Eogan, G. 1968 Excavations at Knowth, Co. Meath. *Proceedings of the Royal Irish Academy* **66C**, 299–400.

Eogan, G. 1974 Report on the excavations of some passage graves, unprotected inhumation burials and a settlement site at Knowth, Co. Meath. *Proceedings of the Royal Irish Academy* **74C**, 11–112.

Eogan, G. 1984 *Excavations at Knowth, Vol. 1*. Dublin. Royal Irish Academy.

Eogan, G. 1986 *Knowth and the passage tombs of Ireland*. London. Thames and Hudson.

Eogan, G. 1992 Scottish and Irish passage tombs: some comparisons and contrasts. In N. Sharples and A. Sheridan (eds), *Vessels for the ancestors. Essays on the Neolithic of Britain and Ireland*, 120–7. Edinburgh University Press.

Eogan, G. and Roche, H. 1997 *Excavations at Knowth, Vol. II. Settlement and ritual sites of the fourth and third millennia BC*. Dublin. Royal Irish Academy.

Evans, E.E. 1953 *Lyles Hill—a Late Neolithic site in County Antrim*. Belfast. HMSO.

Fanning, T. 1983 Some aspects of the bronze ringed pin in Scotland. In A. O'Connor and D.V. Clarke (eds), *From the Stone Age to the 'Forty-Five. Studies presented to R.B.K. Stevenson*, 324–42. Edinburgh. John Donald.

Fanning, T. 1994 *Viking Age ringed pins from Dublin*. Dublin. Royal Irish Academy.

Giot, P.-R., L'Helgouac'h, J. and Monnier, J.L. 1979 *Préhistoire de la Bretagne*. Rennes. Ouest France.

Gowen, M. 1988 *Three Irish gas pipelines—new archaeological evidence in Munster*. Dublin. Wordwell.

Grogan, E. 1995 Excavations at Mooghaun South 1993. Interim report. *Discovery Programme Reports. Project Results 1993*, 57–61. Dublin. Royal Irish Academy.

Grogan, E. 1996a Excavations at Mooghaun South 1994. Interim report. *Discovery Programme Reports. Project Results 1994*, 47–57. Dublin. Royal Irish Academy.

Grogan, E. 1996b Excavations at Clenagh, Co. Clare. Interim report. *Discovery Programme Reports. Project Results 1994*, 58–62. Dublin. Royal Irish Academy.

Hartnett, P.J. 1957 Excavation of a passage grave at Fourknocks, Co. Meath. *Proceedings of the Royal Irish Academy* **58C**, 197–277.

Hartnett, P.J. 1971 The excavation of two tumuli at Fourknocks (Sites II and III), Co. Meath. *Proceedings of the Royal Irish Academy* **71C**, 35–83.

Hawkes, J. 1941 Excavation of a megalithic tomb at Harristown, Co. Waterford. *Journal of the Royal Society of Antiquaries of Ireland* **71**, 130–47.

Hemp, W.J. 1930 The chambered cairn of Bryn Celli Ddu. *Archaeologia Serliana* **2**, 80, 179–214.

Hencken, H. O'N. 1938 *Cahercommaun: a stone fort in County Clare.* Royal Society of Antiquaries of Ireland, extra volume.

Henshall, A.S. 1963 *The chambered tombs of Scotland, Vol. 1.* Edinburgh University Press.

Henshall, A.S. 1972 *The chambered tombs of Scotland, Vol. 2.* Edinburgh University Press.

Herity, M. 1974 *Irish passage graves.* Dublin. Irish University Press.

Kelly, E.P. 1986 Ringed pins of County Louth. *County Louth Archaeological and Historical Journal* **21** (2), 179–99.

L'Helgouac'h, J. 1965 *Les sepultres megalithiques en Armorique.* Rennes. Laboratoire d'Anthropologie Préhistorique.

Lynch, A. 1981 *Man and environment in south-west Ireland.* British Archaeological Reports 85. Oxford.

Lynch, F.M. 1975 Excavations at Carreg Samson megalithic tomb, Mathry, Pembrokeshire. *Archaeologia Cambrensis* **124**, 15–35.

Macalister, R.A.S., Armstrong, E.C.R. and Praeger, R.L. 1912 Bronze Age cairns on Carrowkeel Mountain, Co. Sligo. *Proceedings of the Royal Irish Academy* **29C**, 311–47.

Mitchell, F. 1989 *Man and environment on Valencia Island.* Dublin. Royal Irish Academy.

O'Kelly, M.J. 1958 A wedge-shaped gallery grave at Island, Co. Cork. *Journal of the Royal Society of Antiquaries of Ireland* **88**, 1–23.

O'Kelly, M.J. 1960 A wedge-shaped gallery grave at Baurnadomeeny, Co. Tipperary. *Journal of the Cork Historical and Archaeological Society* **65**, 85–115.

O'Kelly, M.J. 1981 The megalithic tombs of Ireland. In C. Renfrew (ed.), *The megalithic monuments of western Europe*, 113–26. London. Thames and Hudson.

O'Kelly, M.J. 1982 *Newgrange: archaeology, art and legend.* London. Thames and Hudson.

O'Kelly, M.J. and O'Kelly, C. 1983 The tumulus of Dowth, Co. Meath. *Proceedings of the Royal Irish Academy* **83C**, 136–90.

O'Kelly, M.J., Lynch, F. and O'Kelly, C. 1978 Three passage graves at Newgrange, Co. Meath. *Proceedings of the Royal Irish Academy* **78C**, 249–352.

Ó Nualláin, S. 1968 A ruined megalithic cemetery in Co. Donegal. *Journal of the Royal Society of Antiquaries of Ireland* **98**, 1–29.

Ó Nualláin, S. 1971 The stone circles of County Kerry. *Journal of the Kerry Archaeological and Historical Society* **4**, 5–27.

Ó Nualláin, S. 1975 The stone circle complexes of Cork and Kerry. *Journal of the Royal Society of Antiquaries of Ireland* **105**, 83–131.

Ó Nualláin, S. 1978 Boulder burials. *Proceedings of the Royal Irish Academy* **78C**, 75–114.

Ó Ríordáin, S.P. 1941 Structure in Emlagh Townland. *Journal of the Cork Historical and Archaeological Society* **66**, 98–9.

O'Sullivan, A. and Sheehan, J. 1996 *The Iveragh Peninsula—an archaeological survey of south Kerry.* Cork University Press.

O'Sullivan, M. 1991a The art of the passage tomb at Knockroe, Co. Kilkenny. *Journal of the Royal Society of Antiquaries of Ireland* **117**, 84–95.

O'Sullivan, M. 1991b The Caiseal, Knockroe. In I. Bennett (ed.), *Excavations 1990–1*, 40. Bray. Wordwell.

O'Sullivan, M. 1992 The Caiseal, Knockroe. In I. Bennett (ed.), *Excavations 1991–2*, 31. Bray. Wordwell.

O'Sullivan, M. 1993 Recent investigations at Knockroe passage tomb. *Journal of the Royal Society of Antiquaries of Ireland* **123**, 5–18.

O'Sullivan, M. 1993 *Megalithic art in Ireland*. Dublin. Country House.

Powell, T.G.E. 1938 The passage graves of Ireland. *Proceedings of the Prehistoric Society* **4**, 239–48.

Powell, T.G.E. 1941 Excavation of a megalithic tomb at Carriglong, Co. Waterford. *Journal of the Cork Historical and Archaeological Society* **46**, 55–62.

Renfrew, C. 1979 *Investigations in Orkney*. Society of Antiquaries of London Research Report 38. London.

Rynne, E. 1960 Survey of a probable passage grave cemetery at Bremore, Co. Dublin. *Journal of the Royal Society of Antiquaries of Ireland* **60**, 79–81.

Shee, E. 1990 *Irish megalithic tombs*. Princes Risborough. Shire Books.

Shee Twohig, E. 1981 *The megalithic art of western Europe*. Oxford. Clarendon Press.

Shee Twohig, E. 1995 An inter-tidal passage tomb at 'The Lag', Ringarogy Island, Co. Cork. *Archaeology Ireland* **9** (4), 7–9.

Stout, G. 1991 Embanked enclosures of the Boyne region. *Proceedings of the Royal Irish Academy* **91C**, 245–84.

Sweetman, P.D. 1976 An earthen enclosure at Monknewtown, Co. Meath. *Proceedings of the Royal Irish Academy* **76C**, 25–73.

Waddell, J. 1970 Irish Bronze Age cists: a survey. *Journal of the Royal Society of Antiquaries of Ireland* **100**, 91–139.

Waddell, J. 1990 *The Bronze Age burials of Ireland*. Galway University Press.

Waddell, J. 1998 *The prehistoric archaeology of Ireland*. Galway University Press.

Walsh, P. 1997 In praise of fieldworkers: some recent megalithic discoveries in Cork and Kerry. *Archaeology Ireland* **11** (3), 8–12.

Walshe, P.T. 1941 The excavation of a burial cairn on Baltinglass Hill, Co. Wicklow. *Proceedings of the Royal Irish Academy* **46C**, 221–36.

Woodman, P.C. and Scannell, M. 1993 A context for the Lough Gur lithics. In E. Shee Twohig and M. Ronayne (eds), *Past perceptions: the prehistoric archaeology of south-west Ireland*, 53–62. Cork University Press.

Woodman, P.C., Duggan, M.A. and McCarthy, A. 1984 Excavations at Ferriter's Cove. *Journal of the Kerry Archaeological and Historical Society* **17**, 5–9.